IN OLD PHOTOG
BRITA

C000230640

CIRENCESTER
A CENTURY AGO
THE BINGHAM LEGACY

DAVID & LINDA VINER

SUTTON PUBLISHING

Sutton Publishing Limited
Phoenix Mill · Thrupp · Stroud
Gloucestershire · GL5 2BU

First published 2004

Copyright © Bingham Library Trust, 2004

Title page photograph: The Bingham Library
building in Dyer Street, as newly opened in
1905. These buildings are now the town
council chamber and offices. *(W. Dennis Moss)*

British Library Cataloguing in Publication Data
A catalogue record for this book is available from the
British Library.

ISBN 0-7509-3987-7

Typeset in 10.5/13.5 Photina.
Typesetting and origination by
Sutton Publishing Limited.
Printed and bound in England by
J.H. Haynes & Co. Ltd, Sparkford.

Compiled for the Bingham Library Trust.

*The Trust's funding of the research and preparation of this volume is acknowledged
with appreciation.*

Extracts from the pages of the *Wilts & Gloucestershire Standard* are reproduced with the
kind permission of the editor, Peter Davison.

This centenary volume is dedicated to the memory of Daniel George Bingham
(1830–1913) of Cirencester, benefactor to 'my dear old native town', and to those
historians, librarians, trustees, and other citizens who in the past and at the present
time have striven and continue to strive to make the history of the town meaningful
and significant in a fast-changing world, then as now.

A classic scene of boyhood curiosity as this young lad climbs the fence for a better view along
the length of Corin Street, before it became The Avenue and was opened up at this point into
Watermoor Road in the 1870s.

CONTENTS

A Noble Gift: Daniel Bingham stands in the doorway at the formal opening ceremony of the Bingham Library, 21 September 1905. This photograph was presented to the library in March 1934 by J.W.C. Williams and is typical of such generous donations of local historical material added to the local history archives since Bingham's day.

FOREWORD

The commissioning of this centenary volume, and its publication by local publishers with considerable experience in this field, marks a high point in celebrating the life and work of Daniel George Bingham, one of Cirencester's greatest benefactors. The focus for the celebrations has been the period between the construction of the town's Bingham Library, for which the foundation stone was laid on 21 January 1904, and the opening ceremony performed on 21 September 1905.

The Trustees of the Bingham Library Trust are the present-day guardians of a wide range of cultural assets gifted or otherwise endowed by Bingham and those who came after him. So, when the Trustees came to consider how best to celebrate this important centenary in the town's life, they determined on a mixture of events and activities for the enjoyment of present-day townsfolk, and the pursuit of some significant advances in the long-term welfare of these unique assets.

Since Bingham's day, the management and indeed ownership of the library service has moved between various public bodies, and now rests with the Gloucestershire County Council's Libraries & Information Service. For some thirty years, since the present library building was opened in 1975, the county's expert staff and the Trustees have been partners in the preservation and presentation of these collections in that building. In earlier years, this partnership was exercised by Cirencester's former Urban District Council. Over the same thirty-year period, the Trustees of the Bingham Library Trust, as restructured in 1975, have maintained their responsibilities to the town's heritage through these collections, including a long-standing conservation programme for the collection of topographical art, which hangs in the Trust's properties.

However, more needs to be done and in recent years the Trustees have begun to seriously consider their options for making the collections more accessible, better understood and more relevant to town life in the twenty-first century. A gallery space dedicated to showing the best of the material in rotation is in active preparation, and so too are options for digitising the archives and taking full advantage of modern technology to make them available.

Many people, however, will still prefer the written page with its permanent reminder, and so this centenary volume has been planned to bring still more of Bingham's Cirencester legacy to as many residents of the town as possible, and in so doing to increase awareness of and support for the long-term commitments of care, conservation and interpretation, which are essential to the successful exploitation of any local history resource, wherever it may be.

Shirley Alexander, Chair of the Centenary Working Party, Bingham Library Trust
Deryck Nash, Chairman of the Bingham Library Trust
July 2004

A reminder of a long-lost age: two loaded farm waggons pass through the largely deserted Market Place. Cirencester's population was 4,998 in 1831 and around 6,000 ten years later. The Census Return for 1901 shows a population in the parish of 7,536, which included the officers and inmates of the town's workhouse. *(Valentine's Series, 11830)*

INTRODUCTION

One of the joys of living in, as well as visiting, an historic market town is to wander around its streets and buildings trying to unpick the various layers of history which are there to be read by those who look and those who ask questions and seek out answers. The market towns of England hardly ever disappoint in this respect, and in the Cotswolds are some of the finest examples of historic towns anywhere in the country.

Cirencester, long ago dubbed the 'Capital of the Cotswolds', is an example *par excellence*. Today it is still an economic focus for a large catchment area and still offers something of the complete town (by modern-day standards) for its residents and visitors. Examination of the detail reveals a much more complicated picture, of course, which is why it is particularly relevant to look at the town through the course of an earlier period, almost entirely framed within the date range 1830 to 1913, the period of Daniel George Bingham's life.

If modern-day residents feel the effects of change constantly around them, what must our Victorian predecessors have felt? The period studied in these pages was one of substantial change in its own right, not continuous perhaps, but certainly dramatic and long-term in its effects. A simple checklist of major changes or developments in Cirencester over this eighty-three-year period was drawn up as a framework for this study, and records some 150 key events, each in its own way making a permanent change to the life of the town. Most of these feature in the following pages.

This was the great period of Victorian improvements, not least the installation of public services (the town gas works was built in 1833 and the police force established in 1839) and civic improvements (the grand clearance of buildings from the Market Place being largely completed when Bingham was born around the corner in Black Jack Street in 1830). It was also the great era of improvements to the transport network, providing easier links between Cirencester and the outside world. In 1830 the road-carriers and the Thames & Severn Canal vied for the local trade. The arrival in Tetbury Road of the Great Western Railway at Whitsun 1841 changed that balance forever, and by the end of the century Cirencester had no less than two stations and a thriving southern suburb of Watermoor, which largely developed from transport-related business.

Economic, social, public health, educational, religious, cultural and political changes all occurred in considerable measure during this period, and this volume offers just a glimpse at the scale of all this activity. It does so largely from photographic evidence, drawn from the principal source, which this volume celebrates. The story unfolds as a walk around the town, offered in a format that is still possible (and indeed recommended) today, so that the present-day reality of the subjects illustrated here may with interest be checked upon the ground. In some towns, the 'then and now' approach would lead to confusion, cul-de-sacs (many of those) and disappointment, but it is the view of the compilers of this album that Cirencester continues to offer considerable physical links to its past, largely of course through its surviving buildings and streets, and so the resulting experience should be one of satisfaction. See if you agree.

The Roman town Corinium Dobunnorum, undeveloped though some of it may have been, encompassed the whole area of Cirencester and Watermoor combined, and the line of the town walls can still be traced. Post-Roman and medieval Cirencester withdrew largely to a line north of Querns Lane–Lewis Lane (the main cross street of the Roman town), leaving for the eighteenth, nineteenth and twentieth centuries the opportunity, taken up with enthusiasm, to expand southwards to fill in nearly the entire area within the earlier walls. In Bingham's Cirencester, the development of this 'new town' must have seemed almost as important as that in the 'old town', reflected in his own philanthropic actions for the benefit of both.

Much of this development took place during the period under review in this volume. It must have been an intriguing time to watch the growth of one's native town, and in Daniel George Bingham's case to relive that experience on his periodic return visits to Cirencester from his home in Utrecht. He would have seen changes, minor as well as major, that had occurred since the last time he visited, and commented on them in just the same way that local people or visitors returning to the town once again pick up the subtleties of change more quickly perhaps than those living alongside them every day.

So Bingham is a good guide to these things. One of five children of a town tradesman, he would have been quick to spot existing shops closing, new ones opening and other such changes. One wonders what he thought when he found the whole length of Castle Street, between the Market Place and Silver Street, widened by half its width and rebuilt all along one side in 1897. Today it is difficult to imagine that this thoroughfare was until then no wider or more accessible than Coxwell Street, which happily retains the sense of timelessness that befits its seventeenth-century form.

After Bingham's death the First World War was only a year or so away, when things again changed forever, not just on the local scene of his native town. That, as they say, is another story, but it is worth commenting on the fact that today Cirencester spreads over a much larger area than ever before, that the road system is once again the dominant physical feature (and the cause of the greatest friction one way and another) and that the pressure between old and new – in terms of buildings as well as open spaces – remains a key factor in the politics of town government. It is a challenge facing every town with a strong heritage focus.

1

DANIEL GEORGE BINGHAM: LIFE & CAREER

'Your name, Sir, will be remembered by many generations with grateful hearts and your example will shed lustre on the pages of the history of this town.'

Thus did Earl Bathurst propose his vote of thanks to Daniel George Bingham at the official opening of the Bingham Library on 21 September 1905. The 'lustre on the pages of the history of this town' is the underlying theme of this volume, nowhere better shown than in the establishment of improved public facilities, principally the Bingham Library in Dyer Street in 1905, the Bingham Hall in King Street along with a row of dwellings in 1908, and at the very end of his life, a new wing to the town's hospital in Sheep Street. There was much more besides.

Bingham was born on 16 March 1830 in Black Jack Street, the third son of a family of four brothers and one sister. His father, Daniel, was a cabinet maker and upholsterer. His elder brother, Charles Henry Bingham, ran a business as a confectioner and caterer at 12 Dyer Street (now Barclays Bank). In June 1860 Daniel married his cousin Jane Brain, of Kelmscott, and they lived all their married life abroad, except for the summer months, which they spent at their Wiltshire residence, Sunnyside, in Box. But throughout his voluntary exile Bingham maintained a close link with relatives and friends in Cirencester, and contacts and friendships were sustained by life-long correspondence with friends and colleagues.

On leaving school, Bingham became a member of the clerical staff at the Great Western Railway station in the town, not long after its opening in 1841, under its district manager, James Staats Forbes. Forbes was impressed by Bingham's business aptitude and capabilities and supported him in a move to the company's offices at Paddington in 1855.

Forbes later became chairman of the Dutch–Rhenish Railway Company, and moved to Utrecht. In 1858 he encouraged Bingham to accompany him as his right-hand man to help in the reorganisation of the railway. As the *Wilts & Gloucestershire Standard* later reported,

> They found the whole concern there a hot-bed of corruption and inefficiency from top to bottom, and the work of placing it upon a sound, businesslike, and commercial footing was one which might well have dismayed other than young and vigorous men enthusiastically devoted to the recently developed profession to which they had applied themselves.

A subscription list was opened in May 1909, organised by E.B. Haygarth, Chairman of Cirencester Urban District Council, to commission a portrait of Daniel Bingham, on behalf of the town 'in recognition of his munificent Gifts for the benefit of the town and neighbourhood of Cirencester'. The painting, by the Dutch artist Jan Veth, now hangs in the Cirencester Bingham Library, and is part of the Bingham Library Trust Collection. This photograph of Bingham is by W. Dennis Moss, the well-known town photographer of his day, whose work is well represented in this volume. *(W. Dennis Moss)*

After nearly four years Forbes returned to England, leaving Bingham in sole charge as general manager:

> With characteristic and unremitting energy . . . his steady labour and enlightened management triumphed . . . and the whole service and system of the Dutch railways were remodelled, and they soon began to turn the corner of prosperity . . . and the once despised shares stood at a handsome premium. Of course, as was natural and just, Mr Bingham, being one of the men who had sown the seed, participated liberally in the rich harvest which their efforts had produced.

On 13 October 1883 the *Wilts & Gloucestershire Standard*, under the title 'A Cirencester Man in Holland', quoted the daily *Amsterdammer* newspaper of 27 September 1883, which reported events in Utrecht:

Much stir and movement, and especially in the offices of the Dutch Rhenish Railway Co., great activity prevailed here today. Flags ornamented the buildings, and black coats the forms of the entire staff of the company. Work? Nothing farther from everyone's thoughts. Important consultations, meetings and festivities were the order of the day, in honour of Mr D.G. Bingham, who celebrated today the twenty-fifth anniversary of his connection with the Dutch Rhenish. The services rendered by Mr Bingham during a quarter of a century to the Company have been important indeed. To him a large share in the remarkable progress of the Dutch Rhenish must be ascribed; to his efforts the cordiality existing among the staff is in a great measure due. At about one o'clock all assembled in one of the rooms of the spacious buildings, received the hero of the day, offered him their congratulations, hoped still to have much intercourse with him in the future, etc etc, as is the custom on such occasions.

After thirty-three years Bingham retired from railway work but retained an interest in several important commercial ventures in Holland. He was also a considerable landowner, with a house in Utrecht and a hunting box at Schoonauwen.

Mr & Mrs Bingham took an active part in the social and philanthropic life of Utrecht, their kindly interest being especially directed towards English residents away from home ties and influences. In this connection Mrs Bingham has for years been in the habit of having at Catharyne Singel, their house in Utrecht, weekly reunions of the young ladies engaged as governesses or otherwise in the teaching profession, the parties being occupied in needlework varied by recreation, while the religious and more serious side of home life was not forgotten. Mr & Mrs Bingham took a leading part in the provision of an English Church at Utrecht. Bingham gave a plot of land and the foundation stone of the church, dedicated to the Holy Trinity, was laid on 9th November 1911. Mrs Bingham took a principal share in raising the funds for defraying the cost of building and furnishing the church, and many of her English friends, in Cirencester and elsewhere were delighted to send her contributions in kind. Last summer [1912] the Cirencester Friendly Societies' Hospital Demonstration Committee devoted a portion of the proceeds of their annual carnival to this purpose, and provided a carved oak communion table and reredos for the church.

Daniel George Bingham died in March 1913 in Utrecht, 'surrounded by a loving circle of relatives and friends – a rest nobly won by a life of strenuous and useful labour, followed by a leisure consecrated to ceaseless solicitude for the good of others . . . his great desire being to do all he could to better the condition of those living in his old home town, and especially to assist in giving the younger generation a helping hand in their equipment for the battle of life.'

Bingham was a wealthy man, but throughout his life abroad his native town

maintained a warm place in his affections, for no deserving appeal was made to him that did not meet with a generous response. In September 1903 he wrote a cheque for close upon £120 to supply the balance needed for providing the Cirencester bed at the Winsley Sanatorium for Consumptives, and on the same day he contributed £100 toward the contemplated West Market Place Improvement, with an intimation that he should be prepared to give further help when the matter was nearer its practical stage.

But undoubtedly, for the town, the greatest legacy Bingham bequeathed was the building, equipping and endowment of two substantial public buildings, the Bingham Library in Dyer Street (opened 1905) and the Bingham Hall in King Street (opened 1908). He was Cirencester's Andrew Carnegie, born at a time of great change for the town, not least the wholesale clearance of buildings from the Market Place, and he died at a time of approaching international upheaval and conflict.

This volume is presented in the form of a tour of Bingham's native town. The starting point is the Market Place, with journeys out from the core in various directions, returning in each case to the Market Place, the focus of town life throughout the centuries.

John Evans's lithograph of the Market Place, 1814. A local artist and a valuable recorder of the town in the early decades of the nineteenth century, Evans made several drawings of the groups of buildings filling the market space. In this view the two rows can be appreciated, with the large sign of the White Hart prominent on the left. Howse's shop on the right of the church was later removed to open up this area.

2
THE MARKET PLACE

The town centre has been the hub for market activity since 1086 when Domesday Book records 'a new market' for the town. The abbots of the Augustinian Abbey of St Mary were granted the market rights in a charter of Richard I and enjoyed the revenue from two weekly markets, held on Mondays and Fridays, from stalls set up in the wide, open space in front of the parish church.

With time, the temporary stalls became permanent buildings and a tightly packed complex of lanes and houses filled the western end of the Market Place. In 1343 the townsfolk complained that 'the Abbots have encroached on the King's Highway since 1203 and built houses on the market place'.

In medieval times it must often have seemed an overcrowded place, with houses built close up to the walls of the south porch of the church, rows of shops filling the western end, an isolated block of dwellings called The Shambles further to the east; two market crosses (the High Cross opposite the Ram Inn and the Pig Cross opposite the modern entrance to Waterloo Passage), the Abbot's gaol, built in 1221, the Boothall (now the site of the Corn Hall) where the wool market was held, and the parish stocks and the 'blind house'. And to this can be added the day-to-day market activity with the selling of cattle, pigs, poultry, corn and vegetables.

Improvements came with the Town Act, which was given royal assent on 22 June 1825: 'An Act for paving, cleansing, draining, lighting, watching, regulating, and improving the town of Cirencester, and for disposing of certain Common and Waste Lands and Common Rights within the parishes of Cirencester and Preston, and for making drains through the said parishes, and the parish of Siddington.' This meant a complete clearance of the shops and houses in Shoe Lane, Butter Row and Butcher or Botcher Row, along with the Church Tavern standing at right angles in front of the church porch, and The Shambles and town lock-up. All were demolished and their occupants relocated.

Gell & Bradshaw's town Directory of 1820 records some of the businesses operating from this area. In Shoe Lane were Mrs Sarah Hitchings, milliner; William Hunt, cutler; John Sanger, ironmonger; and J. & F. Skipton, watch and clock maker. In Butter Row there were more: John Acott, hairdresser; William Brewer, grocer and tea dealer; Maurice Edwards, pawnbroker and salesman; Mrs Ann Jones, milliner; James Knowles, hairdresser and earthenware dealer; Jane Maysey, fruiterer; John Smith, druggist; and William Stevens Jnr, hardware man, perfumer, toyman, and agent to the Norwich Union Fire Office. Together these trades give a good clue to the character of the town centre at this time, also shown in prints of the period.

The Shambles, a block of buildings in the centre of the Market Place, recorded by John Burden, 1804. This group includes the tiny town lock-up. A large covered waggon stands outside the King's Head. Gell & Bradshaw's Directory of 1820 lists coaches from The Shambles to Bath on Mondays, Wednesdays and Fridays, and to Oxford on Tuesdays, Thursdays and Saturdays.

This view was published in about 1852 by H.G. Keyworth, whose printing office is shown here next to the Ram Inn at the top of the Market Place. Keyworth was in business in the Market Place from 1848 to 1875, and printed poll books for various years between 1852 and 1865. A member of the old Subscription Library in the town, he also founded the *Cirencester Times* in 1856, which he sold on to the *North Wilts Herald* in 1875.

By 1830, the year of Daniel Bingham's birth, the Market Place offered an open vista, with a new road surface, and space to celebrate local occasions and national events, such as the huge feast for Queen Victoria's coronation in 1838. Throughout the nineteenth and much of the twentieth century it remained a busy and thriving centre of family businesses and small shops, providing a full range of goods; the main place for trading, meeting friends, hearing news, buying and selling.

The range of occupations reflects a prosperous market town and the need to be self-sufficient and self-supporting: baker, butcher, grocer, general provisions, beer and spirit purveyors, confectioner, straw hat-maker, boot and shoe manufacturers, dressmakers, plumbers, builders, farriers, chimney-sweeps, tailors, seed merchants, tobacconists, china and earthenware dealers, dentist, surgeons, gas fitters, watchmakers, coal merchants. After Bingham's day the pattern steadily changed, with fewer specialist traders at least in the town centre, although Cirencester is still attractive to shoppers in this respect.

With his father in business in the town, Bingham would have known many traders; the town still required wheelwrights, coach-builders, carriage-makers, general smiths, saddlers, and horse breakers, and could still boast a bill poster, town crier, lime burner, iron and brass founders, and cheese factors.

Some new trades can be found. In 1906 professional photographers included Henry Cherry in Castle Street (at no. 38 in 1906), Mortimer Savory (at 8 Castle Street), and W. Dennis Moss in Gloucester House, Dyer Street. Pianoforte dealers Dale, Forty & Co. were in Dyer Street, and Edward Howard in Park Street; cycle manufacturers Gough & Griffiths were in Gloucester Street and Watermoor Road, and Arthur Matthews in Cricklade Street. More significant for the future was motor engineer Wilfred Bridges, who set up business in Castle Street, responding to this dynamic change in transport.

In the Market Place the upgrading and refronting of individual properties continued, the last complete medieval timber-framed shop, Bishop Brothers on the corner of Cricklade Street, coming down in 1915. Today it is necessary to look to the upper floors to appreciate the range of Victorian shop fronts and street architecture that still survives above the modernised ground floor shops and offices.

A word of caution when trying to locate particular properties: house numbers throughout the town were changed in 1937; so, for example, Mr Cherry at 38 Castle Street in 1906 is not the same no. 38 in the same street today!

The Market Place, photographed in 1912 by John Henry Thomas, whose work features strongly in this volume along with that of W. Dennis Moss. The full benefit of the clearance of the town centre over eighty years before can be appreciated here. Steadily since this time the motor car has come to dominate this open space, but in 1912 it was possible to wander freely, visiting the many small shops, hotels and inns. The Fleece Hotel is on the right and next to it the Sun Inn. Across the road the large Chemist sign indicates the premises of Smith, who moved from Butter Row back in 1830. The Kelly Directory for 1897 records Charles William Smith as druggist and chemist at 14 Dyer Street (now occupied by the NatWest Bank).

John Henry Thomas was an accomplished amateur photographer. Twenty-two volumes, containing about 2,000 images, of his photographs of the Cotswolds were bequeathed to the Bingham Library in 1954. A wealthy bachelor, Thomas lived in Hampstead, London, spending his holidays touring the Cotswolds, staying in hotels at Fossebridge and the King's Head in Cirencester. Among his interests – other than photography and a love of the Cotswolds – were motoring and archaeology. His family connection was with the Old Castle Iron & Tinplate Co. Ltd. Thomas set up a successful wholesale fancy jewellery business in Oxford Street, London. He died at the age of 87. *(J.H. Thomas)*

In this late Victorian view from midway in the Market Place looking back towards Dyer Street, the King's Head Hotel and the Corn Hall are prominent on the south side. The Corn Hall Company, established in 1862, was responsible for building the Corn Hall in that year and the Corn Hall Buildings in 1863, on the site of the Boothall, the town's former wool market. The new addition to the street scene was an Italianate building of five bays and three storeys with a balustraded parapet. A fine feature above the first-floor windows are the symbolic carvings by William Forsyth depicting music, agriculture, commerce and fine arts, plus the Phoenix, symbol of Cirencester. Designed by Medland, Maberley and Medland, the hall was used for lectures, concerts, public meetings and entertainments. It later became home to a library and subscription rooms, the School of Art and a firm of auctioneers. The market function was also maintained, with butter and poultry markets.

The King's Head next door is of similar vintage externally; its three-storey coloured stucco façade of 1863–4 is also by Medland, but conceals a considerably older building at the rear. A former coaching inn, it was a popular venue for dances and formal dinners, attracting hunting and polo visitors and other early tourists to the Cotswolds in the nineteenth and early twentieth centuries. The fine building beyond the Corn Hall was for forty years the home and premises of Charles Bingham, confectioner and pastry cook and eldest brother of Daniel Bingham. (*H.W. Taunt, presented by W. Dennis Moss in 1917*)

The grand sweep of public buildings continues on the south side of the Market Place. Beyond the King's Head is the Wilts & Dorset Bank, today a mixture of shop fronts where it is necessary to look up to first- and second-floor levels to appreciate the unity of a single building, opened in January 1897 as a bank, with shops and domestic accommodation. Other branches of the same bank opened in Cheltenham and Stroud in the same year. Its life as a bank here was relatively short-lived; in 1914 it was absorbed by Lloyds Bank, and banking facilities were merged in the Castle Street premises in 1915.

The bank had been built on the site of the Market House, constructed by the third Earl Bathurst in 1819, which in its turn had displaced an inn called the Oak. When the Market House and adjacent buildings were cleared a large quantity of printer's type was found, no doubt a relic of the printing business carried on by Philip Watkins in the house 'next above the King's Head'. He was succeeded by Mr Thomas Philip Baily, who later removed to premises on the north side of the Market Place and became a well-established Cirencester printer. *(W. Dennis Moss)*

One of the earliest photographs of the Market Place, this view can be dated with certainty to before 1872 because it includes the double-gabled White Hart Inn, a much frequented market house with a back entrance from Cricklade Street, which was demolished in that year and replaced by a shop now occupied by Carpenter's. Dwarfed by its grander neighbours, this timber-framed building was a reminder of earlier centuries. On the right is Alexander and Pumphrey's ironmonger's shop.

Although a poor quality image, this view is important as one of the few to record the Ram Inn, on the right. This courtyard inn, once host to coaches for London, had deteriorated by this date, reflecting the decline of such establishments all over the country as railway travel replaced road for travellers over any distance. It was sold in 1863, and much reduced in size in the following years. Years before, Gell & Bradshaw's Directory of 1820 gave some idea of the business it once enjoyed, listing the long-distance coach departures from the Ram as follows: 'A Coach to Stroud and Gloucester, Tuesdays, Thursdays, and Saturdays at seven o'clock in the morning; and returns Tuesday, Thursday and Sunday evenings, at six. A Coach, Monday, Wednesday, and Friday mornings, at eleven o'clock to Southampton; and returns Tuesday, Thursday and Saturday evenings, at seven, to Cheltenham.' This view is also one of the few to show the Market House, next to the White Hart on the left.

Opposite, bottom: Completing the sweep of the Market Place on its south side, this view also shows the White Hart on the left, the range of buildings across the far end at Jefferies Corner and in the middle the town pump, in this picture a gathering place for local lads. The town was without a piped water supply until after 1882, when the Cirencester Water Works Company was founded, and pure fresh water was taken from the artesian wells which had previously been used by the Cotswold Brewery in Lewis Lane. The water was pumped to a reservoir in Cirencester Park and at 100ft above the level of the Market Place sufficient pressure was provided to reassure the fire brigade that they would be able to deal with any outbreaks of fire. Households could also contemplate the luxury of inside bathroom facilities with flushing lavatories and bathrooms on the first floor.

Copied from the Original (now in possession of Mr Philip Watkins, Cirencester) and Engraved by Edw. Power, Gloucester.

The courtyard interior of the Ram Inn, from a print dated 1719 by William Hogarth (1697–1764). John and Richard Weaver are the proprietors, offering a 'neat choice' of vehicles, carriages, fine wines and secure stabling. The Ram, with its fine galleried inner courtyard, was demolished in 1897 – a sad loss of a fine Elizabethan building. John Beecham, a well-known local artist, used Hogarth's print as the model for one of his historical paintings, which now hangs in the Town Council Chamber. Thomas Wakeman, a London-based theatre designer, chose a similar view for one of seven paintings of the town that he completed before his death in 1878.

The particulars for the 1863 sale provide an insight into the facilities still available at the time in the Ram Inn, which 'contained a bar, coffee room, commercial room, three private sitting rooms, smoking room, large market room, 15 bedrooms and extensive kitchens and domestic offices plus underground cellars'. Additional provision included 'stalls and loose boxes for 30 horses'. The property was acquired by the Cirencester Hotel Company, which also owned the King's Head. Even so, trade continued to fall off and various parts of the street frontages were let off to other businesses. In Castle Street was the Ram Tap; a tap room was a small bar attached to an inn or hotel intended for the use of grooms, ostlers and other working folk. It was still licensed in 1889.

This 1915 view of the western end of the Market Place shows the rebuilt Jefferies Corner on the right and the junction of Castle Street and Cricklade Street. Troops stand on the corner, outside the Bell Inn, during the early stages of demolition clearance of the two shops on the left, both closed, the former J.J. Boulton, drapers, and next door Bishop Brothers, family grocers, tea dealers and wine and spirit merchants. In their place is to be the new branch of the London City and Midland Bank Ltd.

Bishop Brothers occupied an important trading position and had been situated on this site since 1827. W. Scotford Harmer, in his contribution to Baddeley's *History of Cirencester* published in 1924, described the old streets and houses of the town, and remembered that Bishop Brothers 'in spite of much necessary patching and renovation retained most of its original features, including the flat drying place for washed clothes on the roof, which was commonly constructed on houses having no back outlet. . . . The step down from the street into Messrs Bishop's shop showed how the roadway had gradually been raised, for there is little doubt that the ground floors of most of the houses on the south side of the Market Place were originally below the present level.' This state of affairs was also described by Richard Jefferies, sometime reporter on the *Wilts & Gloucestershire Standard*, in his book *Hodge and his Masters* (1880): 'into some of these (shops) you stepped from the pavement down, as it were, into a cave, the level of the shop being eight or ten inches below the street, while the first floor projected over the pavement quite to the edge of the kerb. To enter these shops it was necessary to stoop, and when you were inside there was barely room to turn round.' Harmer described the Midland Bank as 'a building as far removed from the Cotswold style of architecture as it is possible to conceive'. *(W. Dennis Moss)*

This fine view of Jefferies Corner, *c.* 1897, or 'top o' town' captures a scene in town life about to change dramatically. These businesses are shutting up shop prior to demolition, rebuilding and the substantial road-widening along Castle Street, the narrow, almost medieval width of which is apparent on the left, looking down to where W.H. Smith & Son is now. John Jefferies & Son, Nurserymen (no. 141), has already 'removed' to 25 Dyer Street while next door at 140, Stradling, watchmaker and jeweller, is advertising a genuine sale in the buildings previously used as the Ram Inn – the shop fronts replacing and infilling the earlier hotel entrance here. Only J. Hyde & Son, drapers, will survive unchanged. A single market stall is in the centre ground.

The parish church of St John the Baptist dominates the Market Place. This photograph by J.H. Thomas was probably taken from a vantage point in the King's Head Hotel. The *Wilts & Gloucestershire Standard* regularly published a list of visitors staying at the hotel; on 22 February 1913 this included Mr J. Henry Thomas of Hampstead. Two shops on the right are Hamper & Fry, hunt tailor, breeches makers and tailors; and Waldron Griffiths, who in Kelly's Directory of 1897 is listed as pharmaceutical chemist and mineral water manufacturer at 134 Dyer Street following his move from the south side across to this north side of the Market Place in 1892. He was, therefore, the ideal person to seal the bottle buried beneath the foundation stone of the Bingham Library containing souvenirs of the occasion. *(J.H. Thomas)*

The interior of the parish church looking eastwards. Sir George Gilbert Scott described the parish church of St John the Baptist as 'a very fine specimen of the architecture of the fifteenth century, remarkable for its size and lofty proportions'. The light and spacious interior with an uninterrupted view from the west door to the screen and east window is in stark contrast to the early nineteenth-century view in which 'the chancel was separated off from the body of the church by galleries and the organ, dimly lit and warmed by a large brazier of glowing coke'.

In 1765 the church was described as very much decayed, furnishings covered with bat and bird droppings, rotting timbers, walls bulging under the weight of the roof, the nave overshadowed by large galleries and box pews, and a large gallery towards the west window with the town fire engine stored below. Stones falling from the battlements in 1788 highlighted the need for restoration. Led by the energy and enthusiasm of the incumbent, the Revd W.F. Powell, an extensive programme of work, guided by Scott, was begun in June 1865. A local builder, Mr Bridges, was awarded the contract and the work was completed in November 1867, services in the meanwhile being held at Watermoor. The galleries were pulled down, the box pews were ripped out and replaced 'by oak seats of an appropriate nature and character', the altar was raised above the floor of the chancel, the floors were renewed, a new heating system and gas lights were installed, windows were reglazed, rotting timbers replaced, and the organ moved from above the chancel screen. The total cost was £13,706 2s 3d. (J.H. Thomas)

The full range of the east end of Cirencester parish church, as seen from the churchyard. A quiet haven of peace yet close to the Market Place, the churchyard contains good examples of Cotswold-style table and chest tombs, as the photographer shows here. The evolution in architectural styles also shows well in the various chapels. The opening of the ecumenical cemetery at Chesterton in 1871 eased pressure upon space in this churchyard.

The Trust Deed of the Bingham Public Library drawn up on 5 December 1907 states in Clause 9 that 'The Trustees shall also particularly make all possible provision for the bells of Cirencester Church to be rung for a period of not less than two hours on every 21st day of September, being the anniversary of the date of the formal opening of the said Library and the public dedication thereof to the town of Cirencester.' *(J.H. Thomas)*

FROM **G. F. & E. NEWCOMBE.**
TEL. NO. 2Y3.

CIRENCESTER.

DATE AS POST MARK.

C.F.&E.NEWCOMBE.
CONTRACTORS.
CIRENCESTER.

CIRENCESTER TOWN HALL.

PRESERVATION WORKS, 1908–9.

CARRIED OUT UNDER THE DIRECTION OF THE SOCIETY FOR THE PROTECTION
OF ANCIENT BUILDINGS.

Extensive building preservation work on the south porch of the church was carried out by G.F. & E. Newcombe in 1908–9, under the direction of the Society for the Protection of Ancient Buildings. It was essential to stabilise the fabric, which had been seriously affected by the chimneys and flues of the buildings that abutted the porch before 1825. The Newcombe family were well known in Cirencester as builders, contractors, sanitary and building material merchants, stone and monumental masons, with steam saw mills and joinery works in Cricklade Street. A stone quarry on the Tetbury Road and lime kilns near the Royal Agricultural College and on the Gloucester Road supplied local needs. This postcard is a good period example of business promotion.

The traditional Boxing Day meet of the Vale of the White Horse (VWH) Hunt in the Market Place in 1888, with a good crowd in support. Long since removed to the lawns of The Mansion in Cirencester Park, this remains one of the abiding memories of the festive season in the town centre. The VWH kennels were in Cirencester Park. Long-standing trading names in the Market Place can be seen here, including from the left Stead & Simpson (to which property Waldron Griffiths moved only a few years later), Harmer's (Printing Office), Matthews, Frazer & Son (hunt tailors), Wood (tobacconist), and Baily & Son (machine printers), later Baily & Woods.

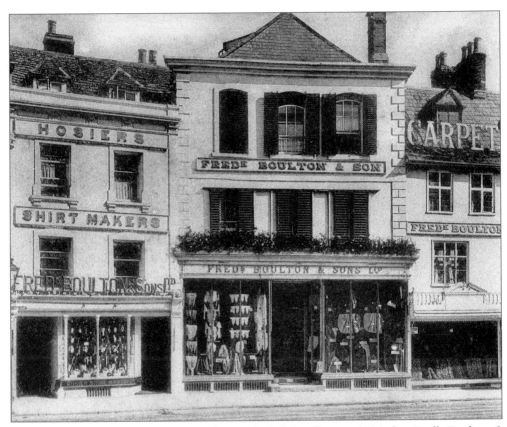

Other trading names in the Market Place included Stradling and Trinder. Fredk Boulton & Sons Ltd is another, drapers, silk mercers, and carpet warehousemen, hosiers and shirt makers at 123, 124 and 125 Market Place, as listed in Kelly's 1906 Directory. In the 1881 Census Returns Frederick was living with his wife and young family at 124 Dyer Street, with five assistants, one apprentice and three servants. This is another form of postcard advertising. *(Postmarked 1905: W. Dennis Moss)*

This charming line drawing of 1898 shows the original façade of the seventeenth-century Sun Inn in the Market Place. Rebuilt at the end of the nineteenth century, it survived as an inn until closure in March 1922, after which the property was for some time the motor garage of Messrs H. Tovey & Son, before becoming Grove Garage. It now forms part of the adjoining Fleece Hotel. A claim to fame of the original Sun Inn was in sheltering King Charles II on his flight from the Battle of Worcester in 1651; in comparison with other town inns and hotels making the same claim – including the Crown and the King's Head – this one seems to have merit. *(Will. Richmond)*

Celebrating the diamond jubilee of Queen Victoria in the Market Place in 1897, one of the set-piece views of celebration in the town's extensive central open space. The town's horse-drawn fire engine is stationed at the back of the crowd for display as well as emergency use. A similar gathering was held ten years earlier for the golden jubilee, and later coronations were also to be celebrated here. Among the spectators, a group on the left have made use of the balcony of Baily & Son (later Baily & Woods and now the Stroud & Swindon Building Society) for a grandstand view. T.P. Baily took over the premises of Philip Watkins and established a business as a printer, bookseller and stationer on the south side of the Market Place before moving to the north side. Other interests proudly announced on his trade card included 'perfume, musical instruments, patent medicines and paper hangings etc'.

The printing works were at the back of the shop, and over the years produced a number of books, pamphlets, directories and guides, including a newspaper. Books included W.K. Beecham's *History and Antiquities of Cirencester*, published in 1842. In 1835 the Permanent Library and News Room was located in Mr Baily's premises, taking in the leading newspapers and periodicals and accumulating a library of over 3,000 books, before it was amalgamated with the Mechanics' Institute and moved to the Corn Hall Buildings in 1863. F.W. Woods later joined the original T.P. Baily, and the business finally closed down in 1985, after 150 years. Throughout this era Baily & Woods supplied the newspapers for the Bingham Library. *(F. Mortimer Savory)*

Above: Peace celebrations at the end of the First World War were marked by a gathering in the Market Place on a damp and no doubt sombre day, 19 July 1919. *(W. Dennis Moss)*

Left: The service of dedication of the town's war memorial cross took place on 31 October 1918 in the Little Churchyard. The cross was an anonymous gift to the town, although it was actually the gift of Mr and Mrs Thomas Kingscote of Watermoor House. Designed by J.N. Comper and built of Clipsham stone, it had a 12ft depth of foundations. This view shows the original fluted column of the cross, which unfortunately was the victim of a violent gale in January 1921; this snapped the shaft in half, bringing down the carved capital, which was 'irretrievably broken'. Mr Comper returned to Cirencester to instigate a replacement, which is the cross as seen today. *(W. Dennis Moss)*

3
THE BINGHAM LIBRARY: A NOBLE GIFT

We are enabled, by the courtesy of Mr D.G. Bingham, to inform our readers, that a contract for the erection of a suitable building in Dyer Street has just been concluded with Messrs Drew Brothers (September 1903). It is anticipated that in about a year this beneficent public project, which Mr Bingham has had so much at heart in the interests of his native town, will be an accomplished fact.

The site chosen for Bingham's 'noble gift' was indeed a prime site, close to the Market Place, a location that at the beginning of the twentieth century could be seen as the last undeveloped property in the town centre, run down and ripe for development. Initially, Bingham wished to remain anonymous, his

keenest desire to keep himself and all personal considerations as much as possible in the background, and to deal with the matter as one purely affecting his old fellow-townsfolk whose welfare he is seeking to advance.

The early optimism did not long survive, the anticipated year to completion taking almost exactly double that time; but it remained a considerable achievement. The project architect was Mr V.A. Lawson, the most prolific architect in the town in the early twentieth century, with offices in Cirencester and Stroud. The existing warehouses and stables on the site were cleared within a few months of the announcement and the foundation stone laid on 21 January 1904.

A Noble Gift
Foundation-Stone Laying

On Thursday afternoon last, the foundation-stone of the Bingham Public Library, Cirencester, the gift of Mr Daniel George Bingham to his native town, was laid, at the donor's request, by the Right Hon. Seymour Henry, Earl Bathurst, C.M.G., Lord of the Manor, and Chairman of the Trustees whom Mr Bingham has nominated for the management of the institution.

It is probably safe to assert that no provincial town of the size of Cirencester has ever received so generous a gift from one of its sons, for Mr Bingham has not only purchased the site and is defraying the cost of the building and equipment of the

Library, but he has also provided a handsome and adequate endowment fund for the maintenance of the institution, so that it may be assumed that the expenditure involved will be somewhere between £25,000 and £30,000.

Self-improvement through lectures and the provision of library facilities was part of the Victorian moral ethos, and for a short period Cirencester could boast two subscription libraries. The Permanent Library and Subscription Rooms had been founded in 1835 in Dyer Street, and the Cirencester branch of the Mechanics' Institution, founded in 1844 for tradesmen and professional men, had a library of 500 volumes, housed in the home of John Beecham in Park Street.

Both enjoyed modest success at first, but public support dwindled and in an attempt to revive interest the two decided to combine resources and move to new premises in the Corn Hall Buildings, newly opened in 1863. The Subscription Library and Reading Room, with a stock of over 3,000 books, offered a range of facilities for an annual subscription of between 5 and 21s, but by 1884 the library was once again in dire straits with funds of only £12. The library's books were sold at auction and only the Reading Room was maintained.

Charles Bingham, Daniel's eldest brother, occupied the adjoining property from where he ran his confectioner's business. He was also a subscriber and regular user with first-hand knowledge of the dwindling affairs of the Reading Room. He encouraged F.W. Woods, honorary secretary, to write to his brother Daniel,

inviting his aid in carrying on the room. Daniel Bingham had previously written to a gentleman in Cirencester asking for suggestions as to what he could do for the benefit of the town, and this matter of the Reading Room led him to entertain the idea of providing a free institution which should fill all the needs of the place. Accordingly, he sent a cheque to clear off the deficit, and asked Mr Woods, in confidence, to look out for a site suitable for the purpose.

In due course Mr Woods suggested the site in Dyer Street . . . and negotiations were entered into with Mr E.B. Haygarth, solicitor to Mrs Robert Brewin, the owner of the property, he also being necessarily taken into Mr Bingham's confidence, and the first part of the site was bought in Mr Woods' name in the spring of 1902, and the remainder of the site was secured later in the year, Mr Bingham having in the meanwhile enlarged his plans. . . . Recently Mr Bingham has also purchased from Mrs Brewin the residence, Dyer Street House, primarily in order that a backway may be secured to the Library premises from the Waterloo, and also in order that if at any future time a further extension of the institution is deemed desirable there may be the requisite facilities for carrying it out.

This foresight bore fruit some seventy years later when the replacement Bingham Library was opened in 1975 in the grounds at the rear, accessible from The Waterloo.

On Thursday 21 January 1904 the elements smiled upon the afternoon's ceremony . . . the walls of the library already having reached a tolerable height. The bells of the Parish Church ushered in the proceedings with a merry peal, and rounded off

Laying the foundation stone for the new Bingham Library on 21 January 1904. In the heart of the crowd Earl Bathurst wields his solid ivory mallet in performing due ceremony. The scaffolding poles are all wooden and rope-lashed together, a world away from modern health and safety regulations. (*F. Mortimer Savory*)

the evening later on in a similarly joyous manner. As the company were assembling, the Town Band, under the leadership of Mr Jacob Carter, played selections of music.

At 2.30 pm. Earl Bathurst was presented by Mr Lawson, the architect, on behalf of Mr Bingham,

with a handsome silver trowel, with ivory handle, and a solid ivory mallet with which to lay the foundation stone, both being contained in a leather case. Earl Bathurst, in accepting these 'working tools', declared his very interesting and pleasant duty to lay the foundation stone of the Cirencester Free Library. (Cheers from the assembled crowd). I feel that today will mark a new era in the history of this good old town and I am sure that today will long be remembered by all present, and will be looked back to with great gratitude by those who come after and enjoy the benefits which it brings. (Loud cheers).

Dyer Street looking towards the Market Place, *c.* 1903, at the time when Bingham acquired Burrows's Corn & Sack Stores and the site of the Bull Inn lying between the Fleece Commercial Inn and Dyer Street House.

The site of the Bull Inn in Dyer Street, later a cheese factor's warehouse, *c.* 1903. By this date it had been for some years the parcels office and garage for the Fairford & Cirencester Omnibus Company. The Bull Inn was the venue for gatherings of the Bull Club, which was (and remains) a gentlemen's dining club with a membership drawn from the business and professional men of the town. Club records survive from 1745, which gives it a claim as the oldest surviving club in the town. Meetings were held in the Bull Inn, on this site adjacent to the Fleece, before the Bull Inn moved further down Dyer Street. W.S. Harmer, a member in 1919, quoted items from the club records including 'whenever ye malt liquor is very bad at ye Bull members went to The Fleece or The Old Crowne'. The club's name is associated with their place of meeting rather than any other connection; whether bull baiting was once part of the club's activities is debatable. Two bulls were bought in 1749, but were they baited or distributed to the poor as meat, as part of the club's charitable purposes?

Workmen line up in Dyer Street, as work comes to an end; the construction of the building itself seems nearly complete – was this the day of the topping-out ceremony? Mr George Drew of Cirencester was the builder; his foreman Mr Cosslett was presented with a gold watch on the successful completion of the work. (*F. Mortimer Savory*)

At this point an interesting part of the ceremonial was allotted to Earl Bathurst's little son and heir, Lord Apsley . . . a huge bottle was confided to his care and duly placed in the cavity prepared for it on which the foundation stone was to be lowered. This bottle, which had been hermetically sealed by Mr W. Griffiths, contained a copy of *The Times* of the day, a copy of the *Wilts & Gloucestershire Standard* for the current week (with a copy of the sheet almanack giving a view of the front elevation of the Library), a copy of the official programme of the day's proceedings, and a selection of current coins of the realm.

The ceremony continued with effusive praise heaped upon Daniel Bingham – sadly he was not present and remained in Utrecht to nurse his wife, who was in poor health at the time. However, the whole town was united in its gratitude for such a munificent gift by a single individual – a successful absentee entrepreneur with a continuing concern for the welfare of his native town despite an absence of over half a century.

The crowds endorsed the gratitude expressed by the Hon. Benjamin Bathurst, MP (and coincidentally Bingham's tenant in Dyer Street House); Mr Haygarth, speaking in his capacity as Chairman of Cirencester Urban District Council; Mr Ellett, High Steward of the Borough; and Mr F.T.E. Boulton, on behalf of Mr Frederick Cripps and the tradesmen of the town. 'Each workman employed on the building received from Mr Bingham a gift of half-a-crown in commemoration of the event', and champagne and light refreshments were served in the council chamber to a representative gathering, Mr E.J. Viner being the caterer. The speeches emphasised the fact that Bingham's 'one great objective was that the Library should not cost one penny to a single ratepayer'. In his charitable bequest, Bingham was following in the steps of other generous benefactors in the town's history: Mrs Rebecca Powell, John Edmonds, successive Earls Bathurst, and the founder of Smith's Charity.

Bingham's intention was to provide

a place for study, for recreation, and for reasonable amusement; a permanent resource for the student desirous of supplementing the education which he has already received in his schooldays; a pleasant refuge for the ordinary reader; and a locality adapted for use on all those occasions for public information and intellectual recreation which become more and more frequent in these days of wonderful scientific progress and discovery.

The style of architecture adopted is Tudor, the windows having stone mullions, with the characteristic labels of the period, and the lights will be filled in with lead glazing. A pleasing feature is the oriel window in the centre of the building. Thus the general appearance of the structure, with its three gables, will be thoroughly in harmony with the prevailing architecture of Cirencester as an old Cotswold town.

THE BINGHAM PUBLIC LIBRARY, HAILED AS A NOBLE INSTITUTION AND A PRINCELY GIFT

The grand opening of the Bingham Public Library took place on 21 September 1905, the second anniversary of the signing of the contract and coincidentally the second birthday of the Hon. William Ralph Seymour Bathurst, the second son of Earl and Countess Bathurst. His elder brother, Lord Apsley, had assisted at the laying of the foundation stone in January 1904, and Bingham felt it appropriate to invite the younger brother to accompany his parents at the official ceremony, which was held in the centre of the Market Place.

Initial expectations were for an opening in October 1904, but significant changes to the internal layout and service provision led to a delay, initiated by Bingham himself, revising, improving and perfecting his great scheme, ably assisted by an accommodating architect and builder.

Bingham himself was able to announce to the assembled crowds that

The building consists of circulating and reference libraries, lecture, reading and smoking rooms, a gymnasium, and a librarian's residence, besides the usual offices required in such an institution. There are over 7,000 books, among which will be found the richest ideas of the greatest minds of the past, as well as of living authors. The reading rooms will be provided with an abundant supply of selected magazines, weekly and daily newspapers. Arrangements are being made for lectures, reading societies, exercises in physical culture, gymnastics, and games, a girls' guild of needlework, and the study and modelling of that most charming and interesting of all instructive amusements, Mr Harbut's system of plasticine.

The opening ceremony for the new library in the Market Place, 21 September 1905.

A crimson coloured platform and enclosure were erected in the centre of the Market Place, around which a huge concourse assembled. As the company were gathering the Town Band played selections, and the crowded Market Place, with the thronged surrounding windows, presented a gay and animated appearance.

The *Wilts & Gloucestershire Standard* also described Lawson's finished product as 'one of the finest institutions of its kind to be found in any provincial town'. (*W. Dennis Moss*)

Although poor quality, this photograph captures the spirit of the day. The newly opened library is festooned with flags and banners.

The town assumed a gay appearance, flags being displayed by all the places of business in the Market Place, St Andrew's ensign floating from the church tower, where bells rang out a joyous peal about noon. The Library itself also exhibited festive emblems. Along the front of the buildings, in bold white letters on a scarlet ground, ran the inscription 'Success to the Bingham Library', while above was the following aspiration expressed in the Dutch language: 'Gezondheid En Een Laange Leven Aan De Stichter', which being interpreted means 'Health and Long Life to the Donor'.

The entrance and staircase of the Bingham Library.
(*W. Dennis Moss*)

The massive arched doorway, fitted with a handsome pair of teak doors gives entrance to the vestibule, a pair of glass and panelled polished teak swinging doors leading into the hall. On the right hand wall is affixed a tablet, finely wrought in copper and bronze, which commemorates the gift of the Library to the town. It was provided by local subscription and bears the following inscription, surmounted by the Phoenix, the arms of the borough.

THE BINGHAM PUBLIC LIBRARY
This Tablet is placed here by the Inhabitants
Of Cirencester as a record that these Buildings
Were Erected, Equipped, and Endowed,
And Presented to his Native town by
DANIEL GEORGE BINGHAM,
A resident of Utrecht, Holland.
The foundation Stone was laid by the
RIGHT HON. SEYMOUR HENRY
EARL BATHURST, C.M.G.
On the twenty-first day of January 1904

The porter's lodge contained

fittings of plate and other necessaries for the supply of refreshments, at cost price, in the way of tea, coffee, mineral waters etc. The fine stone staircase, with wrought iron balustrade, and teak handrail gives access to the upper floors, and is lighted by means of a couple of large windows, which are filled with stained glass, of Dutch design and manufacture.

In accepting the noble and generous gift on behalf of the townsfolk of Cirencester, Earl Bathurst stated:

> He [Bingham] had thought of everybody. He had provided books and lectures for students, reading and smoking rooms for men, sewing classes for girls, a gymnasium for boys, so that it was not only a library but almost a people's palace.

In the time between conception and completion Bingham, observing the development of libraries across the country, had been impressed by the suggestion 'that free libraries should have a lecture room attached so as to interest the inhabitants in books by means of lectures'. Amendments were made to the original building plans: a lecture room capable of seating 200 people was created on the first floor and the Lending Library was moved to the top floor – sixty steps above street level (a climb well remembered by many town residents even today!).

The series of free lectures, arranged in collaboration with the Victoria League, was oversubscribed and proved too popular for the room, and was moved hastily to the Corn Hall. This success encouraged Bingham to conceive the idea of endowing a purpose-built hall; hence the Bingham Hall, which opened in 1908.

There were of course speeches from various people, including Mr Haygarth, on behalf of the Urban District Council – who noted that the Council had been spared the expense of providing a library – and Mr J.H. Legg, on behalf of the members of the Tradesmen's Society. Mr C. Bowly, representing the magistrates of the district, said that

> Free libraries were following very rapidly free and universal education, and the ratepayers of the town might congratulate themselves that Mr Bingham had provided for them what probably before many years were over they would have had to provide at their own expense.

In 1907 a Trust Deed was drawn up to confirm the management of the Bingham Public Library. The Trustees nominated by Mr Bingham were Earl Bathurst (Chairman), the Revd Canon Sinclair (Vice-Chairman), Mr E.C. Sewell, Mr E.B. Haygarth, Mr F.T.E. Boulton, Mr F.W. Woods, and Mr W. Scotford Harmer.

Bingham's gift was indeed 'munificent' and the townsfolk made full use of the many and varied services on offer. But Bingham could not have anticipated the straitened national economy in the 1920s and 1930s, which led to financial struggles to maintain the library, despite the generous endowments managed by the Bingham Library Trust.

Under the Public Library Acts of 1892 to 1919, Gloucestershire County Council was the library authority responsible for libraries within the county, with two exceptions, Cheltenham Borough and the Urban District Council of Cirencester. Bingham's gift had provided a free library, but Mr C. Bowly was proved correct and the Trust found it necessary to ask for help in the form of grants from Cirencester Urban District Council, who were responsible for raising a rate to finance public library provision within the area of the District Council.

In 1960 CUDC asked Gloucestershire County Council to provide the public library service; the book stock of the Bingham Public Library was transferred to the county and the library was renamed the Cirencester Bingham County Branch Library.

The Bingham Library Trust retained ownership of the remaining collection of paintings, documents, photographs and other property (including buildings and investments) donated to the library since 1905 or which formed part of the original endowment. The Urban District Council acted as Trustees until local government reorganisation in 1974, which created District and Town Councils within a new county structure.

In 1975 a new Trust Deed was agreed with the Charity Commission whereby the Town Council of Cirencester was nominated the Trustee of the Bingham Library Trust (otherwise known as the Bingham Library and Art Gallery Foundation). The Trust is a registered charity (no. 311488) and its principal charitable objects are to maintain a collection of pictures and other works of art for display in the town; to provide library facilities in addition to those provided by Gloucestershire County Council; to promote education in appreciation of the arts and music; and to award scholarships, bursaries or maintenance allowances for the furtherance of education in art, music and allied subjects.

Each year the Trust supports a number of projects including the provision of newspapers and periodicals in Cirencester Bingham Library, the microfilming of the *Wilts & Gloucestershire Standard*, the ongoing conservation of the art collection, and the annual peal of bells rung on 21 September to commemorate the opening of the library in 1905. In previous years funds have contributed to the cataloguing of the local history collection and the purchase of a microfilm/microfiche reader. Many local organisations and schools have received financial assistance for a wide range of educational projects and activities, and individuals have been supported with grants and bursaries towards travel and research. The Bingham Library Trust endeavours to fulfil the wishes of Daniel George Bingham in all these ways.

Between 1905 and 1970 the Bingham Library was well served by only four librarians – Mr A.G. Bradbury from 1905 until his premature death in 1909; Mr S.E. Harrison (1909–16), who left to take the post of librarian and curator to Cheltenham Public Library and Art Gallery; Mr H. Tempest (1916–35); and Mr J.P. Jackson, who retired after thirty five years' service in 1970. His successor, Alan Welsford, and subsequent librarians have also held wider responsibilities within the county library services across the east and south Cotswolds as well as in Cirencester itself. The Bingham Library Trust is extremely grateful for the ongoing interest and care of its collections by the county library staff.

To the left of the hall is the smoking room, which is tinted smoke blue, and furnished with marble-top tables, seating accommodation being provided for about twenty persons, while the necessary smokers' conveniences have not been forgotten. Papers and magazines may be brought to this room from the main Reading Room, and their contents enjoyed under the soothing influence of a pipe. Below is a store or cellar for the reception of disused papers.

A stack of copies of *The Times* for 1956 was recovered from this very space in 2004! A surviving receipt from Baily & Woods records the supply of one dozen enamel spittoons at 24s in March 1906. (*W. Dennis Moss*)

The Gymnasium and Recreation Room was constructed at the back of the main building, the yard being excavated to a depth of 12ft. The room is fitted with Sandow's appliances, and regular instruction will be given by Mr Hunt, of Gloucester, and Sergeant-Major Adkins, in Swedish drill and gymnastics. Tables for chess and other games are provided and smoking will be allowed.

There were free lessons in physical culture, given twice a week in the evenings to classes of both sexes. (*W. Dennis Moss*)

The Reading Room, on the ground floor to the right, is a fine, lofty, well-lighted and well-ventilated apartment, with a floor of polished oak blocks. The upper portions of the walls are coloured duck-egg green, which should prove a useful tint to the eyes of the readers. The room is fitted with oak reading tables, and seated with comfortable chairs, accommodation being provided for some fifty persons at one time. On these tables are all the leading London, provincial, and local daily and weekly papers, while the oak magazine rack contains a comprehensive selection of the best and most popular magazines, some of the leading reviews, technical and other periodicals, railway time-tables, and publications giving useful information on emigration and other subjects.

The present-day library continues to offer a range of newspapers and magazines, sponsored by the Bingham Library Trust, in continuing Bingham's original benefaction. (*W. Dennis Moss*)

Opposite, below: The Ladies' Sewing Group meeting in the lecture room. Needlework classes were held on Mondays and Thursdays. In this June 1918 view the classes have been incorporated into a branch of Queen Mary's Guild of Needlework. (*W. Dennis Moss*)

Bingham hoped that the

needlework meetings would be of a social as well as working kind; materials and the instruments to work with, given principally by kind friends and merchants in London. . . . Ladies have promised to play the piano, and the matron will give tea.

On the first floor, occupying a central position in the front of the building, is a comfortable apartment which will be used as a workroom for girls and young women, who may bring their own work with them, or may make use of the materials provided . . . sewing classes will be arranged in connection with which prizes will be offered. The room is also to be placed at the disposal of the Cirencester Chess Club for its weekly meetings.

On 20 February 1908 Dr Lasker, the world chess champion, played nineteen boards in a simultaneous against members of the club and two visitors. He lost to Mr Vincent and drew with Mr H.E. Norris, winning the other seventeen.

On the first floor, immediately over the Reading Room, is the Lecture Room. In this room is provided a platform, lantern screen, and piano for the purposes of lectures and entertainments, and seating accommodation is offered for about 200 people by means of neat folding chairs, fitted with crimson plush covers, for use when desired. In addition to lectures and entertainments, this room will be used for women's and girls' recreation classes, including Sandow's exercises, and the walls are fitted with provision for fixing a number of Sandow's 'Symmetrion' appliances, while arrangements have been made by Mr Bingham for systematic instruction in Swedish drill by Mr Hunt, of Gloucester, a qualified professor.

(W. Dennis Moss)

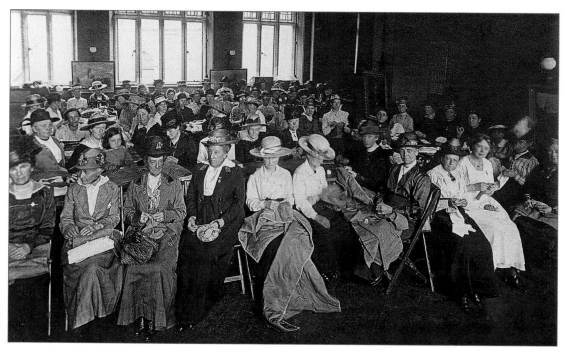

The Lending Library is a spacious and lofty apartment, fitted for the reception of some 15,000 books, and the cases already contain over 7,000 volumes, additions being made almost daily. A conspicuous feature is the handsome polished teak book counter, on which stand Cotgreave Indicators, which show those books that are in the hands of borrowers and those that are still on the shelves.

Self-selection was not available.

The books are classified in the following sections: Biography, Correspondence, etc; History; Travels, Voyages, etc; Religion, Natural Philosophy, Dogmatics and Ecclesiastical History; Games, Sports, and Miscellaneous; Fiction, including Juvenile Literature, Painting, Poetry, and the Drama; Science, Arts, Music, Philosophy, Agriculture, etc.

(*W. Dennis Moss*)

Left: Bingham Library bookplate.

Every book in the Library contains a neat bookplate of exceedingly appropriate design, the work of a Utrecht friend of Mr Bingham, bearing the representation of an old time student at a reading desk in the library, with the tower of Cirencester parish church seen through the open window.

The Reference Library contains about 1,000 volumes of much value and varied interest, comprising encyclopaedias, biographies and the admirable collection of books on local topography and history. The last-named include Atkyns, Rudder, Fosbroke, Marshall and Lysons – in short, a rich mine for the local student of old times and old things.

Also available were the notable local authors of the town's history, including Rudder, W.K. Beecham, K.J. Beecham, Baddeley, and Buckman & Newmarch's *Remains of Roman Art in Corinium* (1850). The local studies collection is still available today, augmented by many gifts and donations of original photographs, documents and published works and essays.

The Fifth Annual Report published in 1909–10 stated, 'It is hoped that in time the Library will contain an almost complete bibliography of the town and district, so that any question of local history and archaeology arising may be answered from one or other of the volumes on the shelves.' Catalogues and card indices produced since 1905 provide the point of access to a broad wealth of local and family history. *(W. Dennis Moss)*

The whole building is lighted by means of acetylene gas, the plant and fittings having been installed by the Allen Company of 39 Victoria Street, Westminster, while the artificial heat is supplied by a very complete and hot water radiator system, supplied and fixed by Messrs Henry Tovey and Son, of Cirencester. The wrought iron balustrade of the staircase and the wrought iron window casements were made and supplied by Messrs T.L. Chew and Sons of Stroud. The fibrous ceilings were executed by Mr H. Frith of Barton Street, Gloucester; and the handsome teak joinery and fitting by Messrs A.J. Arrowsmith & Co. of London.

A Bingham Library book marker, pre-1910, with a good selection of businesses in the town lending their support, while appreciative of the advertising potential.

4

WALKING AROUND
CIRENCESTER

*From the Market Place the walk proceeds along
Dyer Street to London Road.*

A splendid image of the alleyway into the Bull Inn, complete with sleeping dog.
Many properties in Dyer Street had back yards, or 'places' to give them the local name, of
which only a few now survive anywhere in Cirencester. *(J.H. Thomas)*

Dyer Street, formerly Chepyng or Market Street, was comprehensively changed by wholesale redevelopment along much of its southern side in the early 1960s. Virtually all the buildings shown in this view of *c.* 1891 after heavy snowfall, have disappeared, including the double-gabled Ship Inn on the right. A gas lamp stands outside. The Ship Inn was also a lodging house and in the 1881 Census William Wakefield as publican and head of the household recorded his wife, one daughter and three sons, and eleven lodgers, who were listed as a married couple hawking brushes and caps, an iron foundry labourer, a mason, a general labourer, a coach trimmer, a baker, a shoemaker, a labourer, a coal miner and a farm labourer. Six were born in Gloucestershire, with the others from as far afield as Somerset, Nottingham, and Staffordshire. The Ship was demolished in about 1897. Behind the gentleman on the left, Gloucester House and its neighbour survive today. Beyond them the neoclassical façade with columns was Dyer Court, a doctor's home and surgery for many years, and still remembered as a sad loss to the townscape, provoking occasional letters to the paper asking what happened to the columns! Today they would be recycled, but in the 1960s?

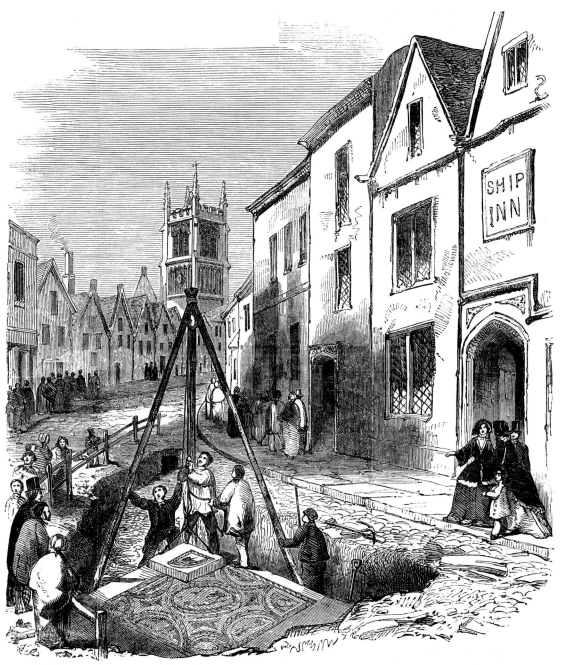

One of the town's most important archaeological finds was made right outside the front door of the Ship Inn, as recorded here in the *Illustrated London News* of 8 September 1849. During the digging of drains several mosaics were found, including the Hunting Dogs and the Four Seasons, now on display in the Corinium Museum. Archaeological interest was aroused by the discoveries and Earl Bathurst paid for their lifting and display in a purpose-built museum in Tetbury Road, opened in 1856.

Roman Remains at Cirencester: In the *Illustrated London News* for 25 August, attention was drawn to the fact that discoveries of Roman remains of the most interesting description had been made at Cirencester during the excavation of a drain which had been opened through one of the principal streets of the town; and that, owing to the praiseworthy public spirit of Earl Bathurst, zealously seconded by the Town Commissioners and the inhabitants in general, great efforts had been made to preserve entire the beautiful tessellated pavement which had thus unexpectedly been brought to light.

Accordingly, notice having been conveyed to the Committee of the Archaeological Institute, Mr Lane (the Secretary) has been actively engaged during the past week in superintending the raising of the pavement, which could not, of course remain in situ, and which is now (from the accumulated debris of ages) sunk to a depth of about four feet below the present surface of the soil; it occupies an area of fifteen feet square, and the design represents beasts of the chase, with a variety of boldly executed masks of Medusa, the Gorgons etc; and the accompanying sketch represents the method which has been successfully employed in removing it; and also affords a tolerably correct idea of the position which the site of this Roman villa occupies. As the work proceeds, other discoveries are daily made, and a trip to this neighbourhood – which, by the bye, enjoys an entire immunity from the prevailing epidemic – would well repay the trouble of any archaeologists.

The Congregational Chapel was a feature of Dyer Street from 1888 until its demolition in 1971. It stood on the site of Archibalds, a medieval manor house, and the land on which it was built was acquired for £900 in October 1886. The new chapel had seating for 537 people, and a school of eight classrooms at the rear; this opened in 1887, the church the following year. The replacement scheme of the 1970s included not only Cirencester's first Waitrose supermarket but a continuing church use on the first floor, surviving until May 1997 when the United Reformed Church joined forces with the Methodists to form the Ashcroft Centre in Ashcroft Road. Interestingly, the Dyer Street building was itself a replacement for the earlier chapel in Sheep Street, which became Apsley Hall and was later converted to form the X-Ray department of the Memorial Hospital. *(W. Dennis Moss)*

Above: Ye Olde Bull Inn in Dyer Street, April 1913. Donald Cole is advertised over the doorway as 'Licensed Retailer of Foreign Wines, Spirits, Beer, Tobacco etc.' and the inn offers 'Good Stabling, Good Accommodation for Cyclists, Skittle Alley & Shooting Range'. The three gabled cottages next door were sold in the 1920s to make way for Steel's Garage (now Gardiner's), and Cirencester historian Baddeley records that this row contained Protherough's blacksmith's shop, an example of light industry behind the domestic dwelling. *(J.H. Thomas)*

Opposite: The lower end of Dyer Street, *c.* 1912, from the camera of J.H. Thomas, who preferred his streets clear of people when taking photographs! Certainly there is little activity in this view, although the buildings make an interesting sweep up towards the Market Place. On the right the triple gables with ball finials date from 1889, a period when a great deal of town rebuilding (much of it relating to properties owned by the Bathurst family) was under way. Dominant on the left are the editorial and publishing offices of the *Wilts & Gloucestershire Standard*, with the overhanging façade dating from 1904. The architect was V.A. Lawson, using local builders, Saunders. The printing works were to the rear, extending back into Lewis Lane. These premises were originally the warehouse and stables of the carriers, Tanner and Baylis. Waggons left every night at midnight with goods for London. In 1817 Mr Baylis lived at The Beeches (later the home of the Sewell family, now a private school); in the hall is a carved mantelpiece depicting an old fly waggon, with barrel-shaped hood and drawn by a team of eight horses.

The *Wilts & Gloucestershire Standard* was established at Malmesbury in January 1837, before moving its printing works to Cirencester in July 1840. George Henry Harmer joined the newspaper in 1851. His 60 years of service included his role as editor, from 1869 until his death in 1911. During this time Richard Jefferies joined the staff as a reporter and wrote a number of local topical articles, which were later published as *Hodge and His Masters* (1880), in which Fleeceborough is an almost exact description of Cirencester.

The value of the contents of the local newspaper continues to be recognised today. Jefferies himself appreciated the paper's long-term usefulness: 'the ponderous volumes . . . the series constitutes a complete and authentic local history. People often come from a distance to consult it, for it is the only register that affords more than the simple entry of birth and death. But even a stranger who took the trouble to turn over the folios would now and then find matter to interest him: such as curious notes of archaeological discovery, accounts of local customs now fallen into disuse, and traditions of the past. Many of these are worthy of collection in more accessible form.'

G.H. Harmer was succeeded by his nephew, W. Scotford Harmer (1856–1936), a member of the Bingham Library Trustees, and a trustee of the Bingham Hall. *(J.H. Thomas)*

The Waggon & Horses Inn in London Road, April 1913, a neat interplay between the recorded scene and the name of the pub! The waggon, a fine example of a local type, belonged to Ampney Mill at Ampney Crucis. The inn was a regular stopping point for carriers and waggoners. On the wall is a poster advertising the reopening of Cirencester Hospital in Sheep Street on 17 April 1913, a nice connection with Bingham, who provided the funds for the extensive refurbishment of the hospital. The Waggon & Horses was subsequently rebuilt to its present form. Next door is Oxford House. *(J.H. Thomas)*

London Road, looking out of the town, 1911. The carriage works of F.W. Constable provided a mix of light industrial activity with newly developed housing areas in Purley Road beyond. On the left and dwarfed by three-storey buildings is the small gabled roof of the Waggon & Horses Inn.

The toll-house in Dyer Street at the junction with Grove Lane, *c.* 1868. This relic of the payment of tolls for use of the turnpike roads survived until 1879, when the tolls ceased to be charged and the turnpike trust was replaced by the beginnings of the county highway administration.

John Evans recorded Gosditch Street and West Market Place in 1816, providing another good, if not necessarily completely accurate, depiction of the time. On the left beyond the abbey wall is the parsonage, opposite the north porch of the church. In order to improve the landscaping within her grounds, Miss Master pulled this building down, having acquired for the parish a replacement building in Thomas Street in 1826. On the right a gabled porch leads through to the Presbyterian or Unitarian church, a seventeenth-century meeting house founded on land behind the cottages. It too was later rebuilt and in more recent times stood empty for many years, until acquired by the parish and refurbished as the town's Parish Centre in 2000.

Returning to the Market Place, the walk makes a circuit of the West Market Place, Gosditch Street, Dollar Street, Coxwell Street & Thomas Street to finish at the top of Gloucester Street.

The account published by W. Scotford Harmer in 1924 ably describes the changes that can be glimpsed in this succession of photographs:

The north and north-west side of the Parish Church has undergone a complete transformation within living memory. Not only was the Church completely obscured by the buildings which extended to the full length of the present grass plot, but outside the north porch there was an outer archway over which dwelt the then sexton, James Haines. This was removed in 1867, being a part of the work carried out at the great Restoration of the Church. James Haines – Jimmy as he was irreverently called – was another Ciceter character. In his day, before the opening of the present Cemetery [1871], the Churchyard was greatly overcrowded, and in his duties as grave digger he used to employ an iron pointed wand to test the ground – after the manner of a cheese-taster – when deciding on the site of a fresh grave. His humour, as became his calling, was not of a frivolous flavour. When he was digging a grave inquiring boys would propound to him the question, 'Mr Haines, who's going to be buried in this grave?' Jimmy would look up from the trench and solemnly reply, 'Nobody as lives in this town.' Whereat the boys would depart wondering why so many strangers should be brought to Cirencester for interment.

West Market Place as seen from the top of Black Jack Street, *c.* 1911. Old London House and Burrows, ironmongers at 6 Gosditch Street, are each advertising clearance sales. Plans were in hand to pull down these shops and open up the area on the west side of the church. In fact, fund raising towards the clearance of West Market Place had been going on for some time; an example was the two-day sale at the time of the opening of Bingham Hall in 1908. *(W. Dennis Moss)*

Opposite, bottom: Gosditch Street looking into Dollar Street, April 1914 – an almost unchanged view today. In fact this group exhibits all the principal façades of Cirencester buildings, the twin-gabled late medieval timber-framed house in the middle, the steep gables of the typically Cotswold house of the seventeenth century nearer the camera; and beyond one of the impressive façades that replaced them in the following century (and so often still disguises earlier structures hidden behind). The austere-looking stone wall on the immediate right is the precinct wall of Cirencester Abbey, a much-patched but still historic scheduled ancient monument and one of the few surviving upstanding remains of the medieval Abbey of St Mary. *(J.H. Thomas)*

A similar view, this time from Gosditch Street, January 1911. The visual effect of encroachment across the north of the church tower can clearly be seen. *(W. Dennis Moss)*

Looking towards West Market Place from Gosditch Street, some time before 1880, this photograph provides an interesting comparison with the Evans print of 1816 seen on p. 60. The shop shown here as obscuring the base of the church tower was The Little Dustpan, destroyed by fire in June 1880. The property was owned by Mr S.J. Hart, and had only recently been extensively refurbished. Objections had been raised at the time and the desire expressed to widen the street and to remove the buildings encircling the north side of the church.

The Little Dustpan formed the extensive furnishing warehouse of Mr George Farrell. Closing the shop at 4 p m. on Thursday, half-day closing, Mr and Mrs Farrell had set off to enjoy a drive in Cirencester Park. The alarm was raised in the early evening by a passer-by, but despite the efforts of the fire brigade and local volunteers all was lost:

This lofty and spacious building, which was at the rear within a few feet of our parish church, and flanked on the south side by Mrs Mace's china shop, and a row of other business premises of some antiquity, is now a completely gutted wreck, and the only marvel is that the whole of that side of the West Market Place was not reduced to a similar condition, as well as much of the property on the opposite side of the street. The burnt premises consisted of a square block of brick buildings, there being four storeys above the cellars, the whole of the ground floor being occupied by the shop, while the cellars formed a depository for oils, furniture and other goods.

By 1897 Farrell & Co. had moved to Castle Street, and boasted 10,000 articles at 5½d each for sale in their general furnishing and hardware stores.

Although undated, this view shows the result of the opening up of the area around the church, as it still is today. A fine stand of trees overhangs the abbey wall on the left and two town postmen pose for the photographer on the pavement, on the exact spot where Gosditch Street becomes Dollar Street, and the culverted part of the River Churn flows underneath the street. Two shops occupy the medieval building behind them. By comparison with other photographs of other Cirencester streets, all the buildings in this photograph survive in use to this day.

The large building middle right was the Capital & Counties Bank, built in 1873–4 by Medland & Son, on the site of Alexander's ironmonger's shop, replacing buildings shown in the earlier Evans print. Ostentatiously Gothic, it has four shields on the façade indicating other branch offices in Cheltenham, Stroud, Redditch and Stow-on-the-Wold. The bank was subsequently amalgamated with Lloyds Bank, in Castle Street, and later became the offices of Cirencester Urban District Council.

Coxwell Street is at the heart of Cirencester's historic core, full still of seventeenth- and eighteenth-century houses of wealthy wool merchants and those who did business with them. It still retains its narrow width. Formerly called Abbotstrete or Abbot Street, it was home to the wealthy wool merchant John Coxwell (1516–1618), after whom the street was renamed. Some of the doorways are dated, including that of John Plot, 'IP 1640', a Royalist whose home was nevertheless plundered by his own side in the Civil War in February 1643, when 'the house full of soldiers and £1,200 taken'.

In the nineteenth century the street was an eclectic mix, including the high status properties of the Cripps family in Coxwell House (now Coxwell Court), and the Hoare family in Woolgatherers (formerly Coxwell Court); the Flying Dutchman public house; the Baptist church; and the carrier William Budd, who operated his flywagon to London every Monday, Wednesday and Friday, and 'goods likewise conveyed to all parts of the kingdom with care and expedition'.

In this view, the Baptist Church is behind railings on the right. This housed one of the country's earliest congregations. At first meetings were held in the cottage of widow Joan Peltrace, with Giles Watkins as pastor (1651). Membership was dependent on baptism by total immersion and the Gunstool Brook, running to the rear of Coxwell Street, was used in the early period. The first church was built in 1671, and rebuilt in 1857 (opened 1858). *(J.H. Thomas)*

Looking the other way in Coxwell Street towards Thomas Street, April 1913, with one of the characteristic rows of gabled cottages settling at disconcerting angles. The building at the far end was the replacement vicarage, bought in 1826 by Miss Master to replace the earlier parsonage in Gosditch Street. On the left at the end in Coxwell Street is Woolgatherers, the home of the Hoare family, important wool staplers with extensive warehouse facilities extending into Park Street.

The 'gap' on the left has a tale to tell: a disastrous fire in April 1890, extensively reported in the *Wilts & Gloucestershire Standard*, gutted the premises of Messrs Saunders & Sons, builders and contractors of Coxwell Street and Park Street, 'resulting in the destruction of property to the amount of between £3000 and £4000. Messrs Saunders and Sons occupied a lofty and spacious building which was in former years used as a wool sorting warehouse, their dwelling houses standing in a yard at the rear, and the yard extends back to Park Street to which thoroughfare some of their premises have a frontage.'

The damage sustained was considerable; not least the loss of the dwelling house, 'an interesting and valuable monument of "Old Cisiter" . . . a perfect specimen of Elizabethan domestic architecture. Some of the rooms were fitted with interesting old oak panelling surmounted by a carved frieze and cornice, while the handsome oak staircase was probably the finest of its kind which the town possessed.' Messrs Saunders & Sons relocated their business to Ashcroft Road and the firm was responsible for building many of the new houses in Ashcroft and Watermoor. *(J.H. Thomas)*

Buildings in Thomas Street, including a classic Cirencester group of triple-gabled cottages with a single entrance off the street; for part of its life this was the Hole in the Wall Inn. Just off the photograph to the left is The Mead, home of Wilfred Cripps, who contributed much to the archaeology of the town. He privately funded and directed excavations in 1897–8 on the site of the Roman basilica, or aisled town hall, thus fixing the orientation of the Roman town of Corinium. Cripps extended his house in order to establish his private museum in a new annexe. In 1938 his collection was amalgamated with the Bathurst collections to form the new Corinium Museum in Park Street.

In this view the tall gable is the Temperance Hall, founded by Christopher Bowly, Quaker, philanthropist and supporter of the temperance movement. He bought the site of a former brewery in 1845 and financed the construction of the Temperance Hall, which opened on Christmas Day 1846, at a cost of £2,126 and with seating for 600. The architect was S.W. Daukes. The hall was to be

a way of demonstrating the victory of sobriety over intemperance, in bricks and mortar. The primary use of the hall was to promote temperance but Bowly also sought the promotion of all benevolent and philanthropic objects . . . to the spread of useful knowledge and, indeed, to any purpose which is calculated to increase the welfare and happiness of my fellow man.

It was used for meetings and lectures organised by the Mechanics' Institute and the Cirencester School of Art; but various restrictive clauses resulted in declining use and a move to the Corn Hall after that facility opened in 1862, for 'lectures, cheap entertainments and concerts', which were not encouraged in Thomas Street. Christopher Bowly died in 1851; his name is also linked with almshouses in Watermoor Road. *(W. Dennis Moss)*

Another fine town study by J.H. Thomas, this time of Weavers' Hall in Thomas Street, April 1914. One of the oldest secular buildings in the town, the hall was founded by Sir William Nottingham, a native of Cirencester who belonged to a family of established clothiers in the town. He rose to become attorney-general to King Edward IV. By his will of 1483 he established an almshouse for four poor weavers in Battle Street, known as Weavers' Hall or St Thomas Hospital, hence the present name of the street as Thomas Street.

A charter confirmed by Queen Elizabeth I in 1566, first granted to the Weavers' Company by Philip and Mary, ruled that 'two of the most discreatist and wisest men of the mysterie of weavers' should be chosen wardens at the annual meeting to be held on the eve of the feast-day of St Katheryne. Apart from this duty of maintaining the hospital, the company had regulations for the conduct and training of apprentices, and for the control of the trade in the town to prevent any unauthorised setting up of 'lombes'. Weavers Hall is still owned and run by an almshouse charity today. In this view Legg's grocery store in Dollar Street is visible. (J.H. Thomas)

St. John's Hospital in Spitalgate (i.e. Hospital Gate) Lane, seen here in a W. Dennis Moss postcard from his Cecily Series. The hospital was founded in 1133 during the reign of King Henry I for the care of the destitute and sick, so that they might pray for his soul and those of his descendants. The building consisted of an aisled infirmary hall of at least five bays (most of which still survive) with aisle walls surviving perhaps as late as the nineteenth century.

At some point after the Dissolution of the Monasteries the recipients of the charity were housed in six tenements, built within and incorporating the arches, which still remain. Late in the eighteenth century the Trustees borrowed enough money to build six new cottages to house the almspersons adjacent to the tenements that had fallen into disrepair, and by 1807 the cottages were in use. It is possible that they stand on the site of the hospital chapel, and their datestone records that they were rebuilt for Richard Wood in 1826. The tenements were largely removed in 1883, although as shown here one remained in the easternmost bay until 1968. Archaeological excavations have since revealed further details. Nowadays a Grade I historic building, St John's Hospital is still owned by one of the town's almshouse charities. *(W. Dennis Moss)*

A view along Gloucester Street, sweeping away from the town, in 1912. On the left is Powell's School. Two schools were founded by Thomas and Rebecca Powell in the early eighteenth century. The Blue School for twenty boys and twenty girls was endowed in 1714; and the Yellow School established from the will of Rebecca Powell in 1722 opened in 1740 after a long legal dispute, catering for forty boys and twenty girls. In 1879, following the introduction of free education in 1876, the Blue and Yellow Schools were amalgamated as Powell's Schools, and pupils moved into a purpose-built school, next to the original school house, which was converted into staff accommodation. It remains a school and the focus of much educational activity in the town. *(J.H. Thomas)*

Sheppard's Place in Gloucester Street is one of the few surviving 'places' or groups of houses clustered alongside an alleyway off the main street. The entrance from Gloucester Street is dated 1694. Similar dates can be found on houses elsewhere in the street. This is a 1912 view.

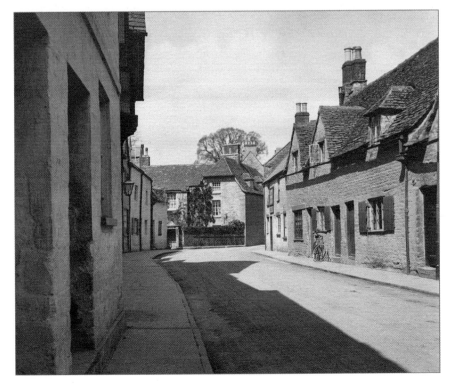

At the top of Gloucester Street, the Old House is dominant, with groups of cottages lining the street on either side, a bicycle leaning outside. The Royal Oak pub is on the right. *(J.H. Thomas)*

This is another classic W. Dennis Moss postcard from his Cecily Series, looking back into town from the top of Gloucester Street, with the parish church in the background. Forming its own community, Gloucester Street boasted a sizeable population in Victorian times, with many tradesmen's premises tucked away at the rear of houses. The street had various inns, including the Royal Oak and the Nelson (both still there) and further down the Loyal Volunteer, which was converted from cottages by 1820. It closed in 1955. In fact, its site is even more remarkable as the home of Cirencester's Theatre, which opened here in March 1799. Its entrance off the street led through into a new building at the rear (cottages were demolished for the purpose) leased by the noted theatre manager John Boles Watson for £10 per annum, plus a benefit night in each season. (*W. Dennis Moss*)

The Salutation toll-house, complete with its gates, at the junction of the roads to Gloucester (to the left) and Cheltenham (to the right). The latter was a completely new road opened in 1827, some fifty years or so before this scene was recorded towards the end of the life of the turnpike system. The toll-house was sold off and rebuilt further along the Cheltenham Road.

A favourite short walk ran along the mill stream from the Gloucester Street bridge to Barton Mill and thence into Cirencester Park or back into town. It remains a pleasant route today. Barton Mill was a significant mill complex until a disastrous fire in September 1923. The course of the River Churn through Cirencester from north to south is complex; this part of the river was canalised to provide power to the mill, after which it flows largely underground through the town to reappear in the Abbey Grounds, where it was also used in turn as part of landscaping features. (*W. Dennis Moss*)

*From the Norman Arch the walk through the
Abbey Grounds leads to Cirencester Park via West Market Place,
Black Jack Street, Park Street & Cecily Hill.*

The Norman Arch, which now forms an entrance into the Abbey Grounds public park from Grove Lane. Often misnamed Saxon Arch, this is the sole surviving gateway and was originally one of the principal entrances into the Augustinian Abbey of St Mary which occupied the site of the Abbey Grounds prior to the Dissolution in 1539. The gateway, for waggons and pedestrians, gave access to the Whiteway and the extensive sheep pastures of the Cotswolds. At the time of this photograph it led into the private grounds of the Chester-Master family home at Abbey House. The River Churn runs under the bridge and roadway in the foreground. *(W. Dennis Moss)*

The Abbey Grounds. In the foreground, in this delightful hay-making scene, is the ornamental lake and grounds of Abbey House, the eighteenth-century successor to the earlier Elizabethan building depicted by Johannes Kip. Trees and ornamental features incorporating fragments of carved stonework from the former abbey buildings survive within a landscape that has been a public park since 1964, providing a valuable green space in the heart of the town.

In the early sixteenth century, before the Dissolution of the Monasteries, the view across the monastic fishponds would have been dominated by two church towers, that of the parish church as it survives today, and the larger tower of the abbey church set to the south of an extensive range of cloisters and service accommodation. The Abbey of St Mary was one of the wealthiest Augustinian foundations, with extensive estates and manors across many counties. In 1539, with the exception of the Norman Arch, the abbey was razed to the ground and the property was acquired by Richard Master, physician to Elizabeth I, and remained in the family's ownership until 1964, when the grounds became a public park and the house was demolished to be replaced by a block of flats. (*J.H. Thomas*)

Above: Abbey House, captured in this *c.* 1900 view by the Cirencester photographer T. Walker, whose business address was in Castle Street. Abbey House was built in 1776 for Thomas Master and set in extensive landscaped grounds. Further nineteenth-century additions to the house included a private chapel and conservatory. *(T. Walker of Cirencester)*

Right: A delightful view of the Abbey Grounds after unseasonal heavy snowfall on 25 April 1908, which was followed by a rapid thaw. This view looks across to the parish church; Abbey House is on the left and its chapel is visible beyond. *(W. Dennis Moss)*

Above: Another view, less easy to appreciate on the ground today but still there in part, and now incorporated within the Abbey Grounds public park. The ornamental landscaping made good use of the inherited features of medieval date. Fragments of stonework including arches, windows and steps were used in the rock gardens and water features within the extensive grounds. *(W. Dennis Moss)*

From the Abbey Grounds a path leads through into West Market Place and the top of Black Jack Street. The demolition of businesses in West Market Place opened up the view to the base of the tower of the parish church. The improvements had been a long-cherished project. This postcard printed by W.D. Moss in September 1913 shows the west door from St John Street, alias Black Jack Street, revealed for the first time for several centuries. *(W. Dennis Moss)*

Here is the same view before clearance, with the products of master butcher Alfred Tranter on open display. Here he employed eight men and two boys before he began trading under the name of Cole & Tranter, following a move to Castle Street.

The derivation of the name Black Jack Street has attracted persistent conjecture and various theories. Medieval documents refer to Temple Street in 1459 corresponding to the length of street extending from the bottom of Cecily Hill via Park Street and Black Jack Street to the church. By 1509 Temple Street had been changed to St John's Street, taking its name from the church dedication to St John the Baptist.

Among the suggestions for the name Black Jack Street is reference to the statue of St John in the niche in the north-west angle of the tower, smoke-blackened over the centuries from the cluster of houses that encircled the church until the late nineteenth century, and of course in one memorable fire in 1880 at The Little Dustpan. Alternatively, a black jack was a leather bottle for ale, indicating a link with an inn; the Crown stood (and still stands) on the street corner here. Another idea is a link with a blacksmith based in the street.

Several residents in the nineteenth century felt it an unfashionable name and businesses chose to use St John's Street, leading inevitably to confusion, which was resolved when in 1887 the Local Board recommended the use of Black Jack Street. But Mortimer Savory and Dennis Moss persisted, and several postcards record St John Street as late as 1913. (W. Dennis Moss)

A similar view of Black Jack Street from further down the street and dating from April 1913. Here are some long-established businesses, including on the left under the awning Jesse Smith, family butchers, sausage makers and bacon curers. Beyond is Daniel Cowley, carpenters, a long-established business, and for many years an undertakers. The buildings beyond are another example of rebuilding, this time in 1909. At the top of the street is a hanging sign: 'W.H. Smith & Son, Pictures'. Opposite on the right is the Old Crown Inn, on the corner with West Market Place. Other buildings on this side have since been demolished, to provide enlarged access to the post office yard. On the church tower the statue of St John is visible in its niche; it was removed as unsafe in the 1960s. *(J.H. Thomas)*

Old houses on the corner of Black Jack Street with Silver Street, a few years before rebuilding the whole of this group. This is an early view of about 1864–5, and includes the home of Daniel George Bingham – the gabled house in Black Jack Street. This and the other largely timber-framed buildings were demolished and rebuilt in 1868–9 by William Lennox Bathurst, fifth Earl Bathurst, with A.W. Maberley as architect. The large and dominant Abberley House, now part of Corinium Museum, is on the left. *(J.H. Thomas, copying an earlier photograph)*

The same scene years later and moving the camera round into Silver Street. Much the same view is afforded today, but with considerably more traffic! The corner shop was a fancy repository, kept by the Misses Marsh. *(W. Dennis Moss)*

At the junction of Park Street and Thomas Street with Cecily Hill. On the left is Monmouth House, an L-shaped house of the fifteenth and sixteenth centuries; on its wall is a sign 'To Swimming Bath'. This open-air pool was one of the first built in the country, opening in 1870. Beyond is the Old Vicarage facing up Coxwell Street. Flowing under the road at this junction is Gumstool or Gunstool Brook, a branch of the River Churn, which until 1854 was an open watercourse. It ran parallel to Coxwell Street through the rear gardens and under Dollar Street until it reached the Abbey Grounds. A serious outbreak of cholera and concerns for public health resulted in the culverting of this stretch of the stream from the bridge at the bottom of Cecily Hill. Until then the stream adjacent to the bridge here provided a convenient watering spot for horses for many years, and may also have been the site of the 'goging stool' or ducking stool. The tall warehouse on the right was used for storing wool and formed part of the premises of the Hoare family of Coxwell Court. (*W. Dennis Moss*)

A similar view, from Cecily Hill, showing the Tontine Buildings on the left and the small sweet shop, sometime Jackson's and later Clatworthy's.
(*J.H. Thomas*)

Cecily Hill, or Ciceley Hill as this unidentified photographer spells it, showing on the right the complete group of ten cottages with one central arch forming the Tontine Buildings of 1802. This group was built by Thomas Bayley Howell, an unsuccessful candidate in local elections of 1796 and 1802. Beyond and partially obscured by the tree is Cecily Hill House. Then, as now, this road is impressive in scale and width, leading up to the gates of Cirencester Park (the park, not the house).

A view across the town from the roof of the Barracks in Cecily Hill. As ever, the parish church stands out, but in this view so too do the chimneys of Cirencester Brewery in Cricklade Street, and the rear view of The Mansion, Cirencester Park on the right. Until 1818 Cecily Hill was the principal turnpike road leaving the town for Stroud via Park Corner. Earl Bathurst diverted the route and the line from Tetbury Road to Sapperton was adopted, skirting the edge of the park. (*W. Dennis Moss*)

Cirencester Park gates, with lodges either side and the Barracks, an impressive group at the entrance to the park at the top of Cecily Hill. This view is from inside the Park. The eighteenth-century gates were brought from Carshalton in Surrey and erected in about 1856. The Barracks were built in 1856, in a castellated gothic style, to serve as the armoury and headquarters for the Royal North Gloucestershire Militia, which became the 4th Battalion of the Gloucestershire Regiment. In 1924 Harmer reported that the Armoury 'occupies the site of a rookery of old cottages, which were pulled down to make way for it'.

At street level the scale and proximity of Cirencester Park is not fully appreciated, the yew hedge and high wall obscuring all sight of the house. A climb to the top of the church tower affords the best view and rewards the effort. In the foreground Black Jack Street and Park Street lead down to the park entrance. Behind the house Queen Anne's Ride is clear; and on the right the Broad Ride, a popular walk for local people for many years. This photograph is from before 1938, when the Corinium Museum was built at the rear of Abberley House.

The Mansion, or Cirencester House, as seen from the Home Park. This was largely rebuilt in 1715 by Allen first Earl Bathurst, with further remodelling in the early nineteenth century. The first house on the site was built for Sir John Danvers, c. 1580, and Bathurst demolished the wings of this Elizabethan house to give a long, thin rectangular house. Work by Robert Smirke in 1830 included the remodelling of the east front. (W. Dennis Moss)

Cirencester Park is highly regarded as an early eighteenth-century landscape park with extensive woodlands over some 3,000 acres. It also has a number of follies of different architectural styles, set into the park landscape as distinctive features. The Hexagon of *c*. 1736 is one such, a six-sided structure, occasionally misnamed the Octagon. Set back slightly from the Broad Ride, it commands a view down the length of Windsor Walk which connects to the Tetbury Road. For generations it has been a favourite destination for those who want a short walk in the park. *(W. Dennis Moss)*

Further into the park at Seven Rides is Pope's Seat. The influence of the poet Alexander Pope in the landscaping of the park with the first Earl Bathurst is commemorated in the naming of this folly, a delightful shallow building with iron-bound seats. Its design is neoclassical with pedimented arches, rusticated stonework, niches and ball finials on either side. In this area of the park are other buildings such as Ivy Lodge, the Square Tower and the Woodhouse, functional in use but designed as folly features. *(W. Dennis Moss)*

The Round House, another of the attractive buildings clustered around Seven Rides in Cirencester Park. The turnpike road to Stroud ran past here until 1818.

Alfred's Hall is perhaps the most mysterious of the park's follies, and an important early example. Designed by Earl Bathurst with Alexander Pope in 1721, it was enlarged in 1732 and has later nineteenth-century alterations; it is probably the first Gothick sham ruin to be built in England, and incorporates fragments of Sapperton manor house. It was a popular venue for outings from the town, including the Primrose League and other groups, for teas held in the great hall. (*W. Dennis Moss*)

From the Market Place walking west down Castle Street to Tetbury Road & Sheep Street.

The Bell Inn at the corner of Castle Street with Cricklade Street. Unusually for Cirencester, this inn is of brick, which was subsequently rendered. The landlord at the time of this photograph was Frederick Wicks.

Opposite the Bell, Jefferies Corner of the Market Place, with the Ram Inn beyond in Castle Street. Messrs John Jefferies & Sons were a long-established firm of nurserymen and nationally renowned growers of roses. In a July 1881 edition the *Wilts & Gloucestershire Standard* exhorted the residents of the town to walk to Siddington to view their nursery and the brilliant display of blooms: 'a magnificent collection of roses, the "Queen of Flowers"'.

At the opposite end to Jefferies, on the old north side of Castle Street at the junction with Silver Street in 1890, were the Great Western Refreshment Rooms, offering 'Hot Dinners Daily from 12 o'clock until 3 p.m., Tea and Coffee always ready, Chops and Steaks on the shortest notice. Good Accommodation for Cyclists. Commercial Rooms Upstairs. Well-Aired Beds. R. Robinson Proprietor' – a fine piece of comprehensive advertising. In 1894 this was known as the Great Western Coffee Tavern. Next door is J. Handley, clothier, hatter and outfitter who moved into the Market Place in 1895, in advance of the redevelopment. Along Castle Street the flag of the British Workman coffee tavern hangs from a window of the former rooms of the Ram Inn.

Earl Bathurst commissioned John Birch, a London architect, to design a new range of buildings for the northern side of Castle Street. The shops and offices, dated 1896, form a two-storey neo-Tudor block, with a datestone in the gable with the initial B for Bathurst and the date 1897. This was a major redevelopment from the corner of the Market Place, extending to the junction with Silver Street, and included doubling the width of the roadway. The nurserymen, John Jefferies & Son, returned to their corner site while at the other end the post office moved into the purpose-built premises which it still occupies. Local author J. Arthur Gibbs, in his book *A Cotswold Village* published in 1898, wrote: 'It should be noted that some of the new buildings in this town, such as that which contains the post office, have been erected in the best possible taste . . . we have never seen modern architecture of greater excellence than these Cirencester houses. They are as picturesque as houses containing shops possibly can be.'

A grand façade of buildings, including the municipal offices in the centre. In 1876 the Local Government Board was created to take over the duties of the Town Commission which had been established in 1825, largely to oversee the clearance of the Market Place. The Local Government Act of 1894 created Cirencester Urban District Council, which met in the old town hall over the south porch of the church for the first five years of its existence. In 1899 it was able to move to the newly built chamber in Castle Street, and occupied the offices until 1932 when it moved to Gosditch Street. *(W. Dennis Moss)*

Cirencester Urban District Council members outside the Council Chambers in Castle Street, 1912. Eighteen members and officers are named: G. Lafford (Deputy Clerk), R.W. Ellett (Clerk), Ernest Newcombe. T. Hibbert (Surveyor), E.C. Sewell, J. Habgood, S. Boulton, J.M. White, E.J. Mead, J. Tyrrell, O.J. Fowler (Chairman), E.B. Haygarth (Vice-Chairman), S. Clappen, W.G. Bridges, W. Cole, E.J. Burge, A.J. Mattews and H.T. Gardner. Among this group are prominent and successful businessmen with wide-ranging interests in many of the town's public organisations.

The etched business name in the window glass also shows that this was the office of another significant figure. As a chartered civil engineer and architect, the achievements of Vincent Alexander Lawson (1861–1928), AMICE, FIAA are an important part of the story of Cirencester during the Bingham period. He completed a great deal of work in and around the town, much of which can still be appreciated today: 'as an engineer and architect he has left behind him many proofs of his professional ability both in the Cirencester and Stroud districts, as well as further afield'.

Lawson trained as an engineer before turning to architecture. He became President of the Incorporated Association of Architects and Surveyors, and had offices in Stroud and Cirencester. Among his contributions to town life were his honorary roles as Honorary Architect to Cirencester Memorial Hospital; as a Trustee of Bingham Public Library in 1915, appointed on the death of Mr E.B. Haygarth; and as one of the original founders of the Cirencester Young Men's Christian Association (1917–18).

His work for Bingham included the Bingham Public Library (1905), the Bingham Hall and cottages (1908), and the extension to the Cottage Hospital (1913). Other public and commercial commissions were the conversion of Apsley Hall in about 1921 to create the Memorial Hospital, the *Wilts & Gloucestershire Standard* Offices in Dyer Street of 1904, and the very un-Cotswold style of the Midland Bank, with Thomas B. Whinney (1915). There were other projects for council houses, various shops and business premises, including cottages in Gloucester Street (1902); Bowly Almshouses, additions of 1911; and the early Siddington Road Council Houses, 1912. The refurbishment for W.H. Smith in Castle Street (1902, 1924-5) and the renovation of the Royal Agricultural College, reopened 1924, are also notable.

For other private clients, he designed the Sarawak Museum for Rajah Brooke at Chesterton House, and additions to the house for Sir Charles Brooke (1902, 1913); Oakley Hall for Lord Grantley (1903); and Watermoor House, including the chapel for Thomas Kingscote (1908).

Finally, but not least in this impressive list are some new houses for clients: Stratton Place (1900–10), Waterton House (1901), Daglingworth Place (1907), Calmsden Manor (1924-5), and alterations to Rendcomb Park (1920). *(W. Dennis Moss)*

The Globe Temperance Hotel on the corner of Silver Street and Castle Street. As with many properties, a look above the modern shop windows of plate glass will reveal the earlier façade and so help to appreciate the changes at ground level. The Temperance Hotel, with its immediate neighbour Camden House in Silver Street, survived the 1897 redevelopment of this north side of Castle Street, while the Great Western Refreshment Rooms and Handley's were cleared to be replaced by the post office. The Globe was run by Mrs Wilton from 1896 to 1900, when she opened up a restaurant in the Market Place. *(W. Dennis Moss)*

This view across Castle Street shows a range of businesses, including the King's Arms and the Black Horse inns (both today incorporated into one pub) and the shop that was later enlarged to become Bridges Garage. The plaster motifs of the Vampage family survive beneath the bay windows. *(W. Dennis Moss)*

More rebuilding in progress, this time the enlargement of Bridges Garage, with its large hanging sign as 'sole agent for Mercedes, Daimler, Sunbeam cars'. The windows also advertise the stocking of Dunlop and Michelin tyres. Bridges Garage was founded in 1901 by Wilfred George Bridges and began trading from these premises in Castle Street. The property was originally, in the fifteenth and sixteenth centuries, the home of the Vampage family, with fine half-timbered façade and projecting first-floor windows. Bridges also had a coachworks in Cricklade Street, building bodies for Sunbeam and Rolls-Royce; and the firm later expanded to include agricultural machinery. The company moved further down Castle Street in 1919.

This enlargement involved the demolition of the adjoining property of W.P. Paish, Cooperage and Brush and Broom Dealer. The roof tiles are being removed and carefully stacked for re-use. The family of Paish were well known as basket-makers. An advertisement in the *Wilts & Gloucestershire Standard* in July 1881, inserted by Daniel Paish, reports the firm was established in 1802, Basket & Sieve Maker & Cooperage, of 77 Castle Street and 62 Gloucester Street.

Daniel Paish returns his most sincere thanks to the Nobility, Clergy, Gentry and his Patrons generally for the kind and liberal support that has been accorded to his late father and himself from the commencement of the present century, and begs to announce that he has purchased the Good-will and Stock-in-Trade of the business carried on by Mr Frederick Pepperell in Castle Street for the past thirty years. With increased facilities for business, Daniel Paish respectfully solicits a continuance of public favour, which it will be his constant study to deserve. Lounging, Garden and other chairs made to order on the Shortest Notice. Baskets of Every Description.

The two properties are now W.H. Smith, after conversion work in 1924 by V.A. Lawson. The neighbouring property to the right was the home and business premises of the Beecham family for many years, trading as 'Plumber, house decorator, artists' colourman and picture frame maker.' (*W. Dennis Moss*)

Looking along Castle Street away from the Market Place, before 1901. The goods of Paish the basket-maker are much in evidence hanging from their display rail. Without any traffic to hinder the view, the gentle sweep of lower Castle Street can be appreciated. On the left is the home of John Beecham (1813–82), an accomplished signwriter and heraldic artist, whose family ran a decorating business. John Beecham was a painter of romantic historical scenes of the town, many of which survive to this day. He painted *The Attack on Lord Chandos' Coach*, *The Arrival of the Coach at the Ram Inn*, *The Surrender of Cirencester Abbey*, *The Distribution of Bucks and Does*, and *King Edward Celebrating Christmas at St John's Hospital* – all large canvases full of interesting historical interpretation. He was also a competent lithographer. Beecham set up business in Castle Street in 1865, moving from Dunstall House in Park Street; his new premises remained in the family until 1912. Here plumbing, glazing and general house decorating were offered, along with the supply of artists materials and picture framing. The hall and stairwell at 76 Castle Street were of a size to exhibit the larger paintings, with open access to townspeople. The paintings were later moved and displayed in the Bingham Library and remain today in the care of the Bingham Library Trust. A number are displayed in the Town Council Chamber. *(probably H.W. Taunt)*

On the right is another of Cirencester's fine buildings, albeit a little grimy in this view. Nos 14 and 16 Castle Street were built for a wool merchant in about 1730, the finest Palladian example in the town. The premises became a bank in about 1790, one of two private banks formed in Cirencester at this time. This was Messrs Pitt, Croome, Bowly & Brown's Bank – commonly known as Bowly's Bank; in 1836 it was absorbed by the County of Gloucester Bank Ltd, which continued to offer services until absorbed by Lloyds Bank in 1897. By 1932 all the activities of Lloyds Bank were concentrated in Castle Street, and remain so today.

On the left, the new owner after the Beecham family of 76 Castle Street was the Cirencester Conservative Association Working Men's Benefit Society, established in 1890 with the purpose of offering some protection for agricultural and other working men not covered by other benefit in times of sickness. It held its first meeting in the Bell Inn in the Market Place in 1889 before moving to Park Lane and thence to Castle Street, after suitable alterations in 1912. The society became a well-established feature of town and district life, with branches across the Cotswolds and beyond. Removed only in recent years to a new location in Dyer Street, the society still flourishes as the Cirencester Friendly Society. *(probably H.W. Taunt)*

In Castle Street, looking towards the Market Place, pre-1897. The Great Western Refreshment Rooms can be seen beyond the bank. The railings on the right indicate the garden frontage of Elm Court, which was demolished in the 1890s.

Elm Court in Castle Street was the home of the Bowly family, a leading Cirencester business family and owners of a brewery. Demolished in the 1890s, Elm Court was replaced by Castle Buildings, an austere row of shops. John Beecham's house is on the left.

Castle Street in 1913, full of activity and trading in progress. On the right is the Noah's Ark, a general dealer's named after the wooden model hanging on the wall. Goods for sale range from buckets and baskets to postcards. The property on the left is the Cosy Tea Room, newly opened in 1912. The shop was run by Hobbs, a baker and confectioner's next door. Further up, emblazoned across the building is the name Pullan, a cycle and gun manufacturer, operating from premises next to W.D. Moss's photographic studio. *(W. Dennis Moss)*

Opposite, bottom: Castle Street, including Castle Buildings, in the late 1920s/early 1930s. This photograph is notable in that it shows the Gainsborough House Studio of W. Dennis Moss, whose business offered a range of services: 'Photographic Artist & Miniature Painter; Framing, Gilding & Re-gilding; Oil Paintings re-cleaned and re-lined; Oil Engravings cleaned and restored; Photographs Mounted and Titled'. His sign hangs outside the premises, and Moss's car is parked on the kerb. The shops beyond include Legg's (cabinet maker), Raymond Tranter (family & pork butcher), and Charles Trotman (grocer). Bridges Garage is further down the street. Moss took over his business from F. Mortimer Savory in the early years of the twentieth century. *(W. Dennis Moss)*

J.H. Thomas's photographic record of the fine run of tall gabled buildings in this same part of Castle Street, including Farrell's house furnishers and hardware merchants (who had moved here from West Market Place), the Noah's Ark, and Kittow's hairdresser and umbrella maker. In further replanning in more recent years, the name Farrell Close is a record of one of these long-standing businesses. The town's police station and Magistrates Court is on the extreme left. (*J.H. Thomas*)

Opposite, bottom: A fine view from Tetbury Road, *c.* 1925, showing the increase in traffic by this date – and a wandering dog! Prominent at the road junction is the police station and Petty Sessional Court of 1858/9. Another Cirencester building by James Medland, this also housed a room for magistrates and a residence for the superintendent and his staff. It was enlarged in the 1880s with the County Court and Magistrates Court moving here from the town hall. A long row of cottages had previously stood on this site, including one 'with a battlemented parapet, after the fashion of the toll-house at Grove Lane'. The town's earlier police station was in Gloucester Street, in rented premises opposite the Duke of York Inn. On the right is the Marlborough Arms, a Stroud Brewery pub, with a horse-drawn cart outside.

Looking from Castle Street towards Tetbury Road, with more businesses in this important commercial street. The projecting sign, Hairdresser & Umbrella Maker, is for John Kittow, a long-established firm, and another of Cirencester's characters according to W. Scotford Harmer. He was a barber and in later life Town Crier. Born in The Shambles in 1818, he died in 1916 aged 97, as 'Cicester's then oldest inhabitant'. At the foot of Tetbury Road is the Bathurst Museum of Roman Antiquities (complete with porter's lodge) opened here in 1856, displaying antiquities discovered in the town. (*W. Dennis Moss*)

'Near the GWR station, Cirencester' on the corner of Castle Street and Tetbury Road with Sheep Street and Park Lane. On the left can just be seen another Cirencester pub, the Three Compasses, shown here before it was rebuilt in 1919 by Sidney Gambier Parry. Next door is Fredk Bond, cabinet maker. The railings and hoardings mark the approach to the Great Western Railway station.

Many people would not recognise this row of cottages in Sheep Street, which fell victim to one part of the house clearances and street-widening schemes associated with the new Cirencester ring road and bypass in the 1960s and '70s. This view in April 1914 is towards the old Tetbury Road from outside the hospital gates in Sheep Street. The station yard is behind the cottages, and Apsley Hall is off to the left. (*J.H. Thomas*)

Opposite, bottom: The Great Western Railway station, terminus of a branch line from Kemble, opened in May 1841 and closed in 1964. This view is from the station yard with the platform out of picture to the right. Staff pose in front of the parcels office, which was later rebuilt. The tall narrow station building was built to a design by Isambard Kingdom Brunel, and was the workplace of the young Daniel George Bingham before his transfer to Paddington, hub of the GWR. The station building survives today, albeit without an alternative use, and the rest of the site is a car park. (*postmarked 1904; Cherry of Castle Street, Cirencester*)

The Museum of Roman Antiquities opened at the foot of Tetbury Road in 1856 to house and display the Bathurst family collection of antiquities from Cirencester, seen here in a print from the *Illustrated London News*. It was inspired by the discovery of mosaics in Dyer Street in 1849. The *Wilts & Gloucestershire Standard* for 22 February 1913 reported,

During the year 1912 the number of persons who visited the Museum was 1,392. Parties varying in number from 92 to single units paid visits on 162 days. The month of August was highest with 475, and January with 16 the lowest. The most on a single day was 101 on 27 August.

The Bathurst collection of antiquities was amalgamated with the Cripps collection in 1938, and transferred to form the newly built Corinium Museum in Park Street.

Interior of the museum, *c.* 1930. Mosaics adorn the floors and other objects are displayed around the walls in this single room, an impressive space and an early example of a privately funded purpose-built museum building. (*W. Dennis Moss*)

The main building of the Royal Agricultural College presents an impressive façade on Tetbury Road, about a mile out of town. Opened in 1846, it was the earliest agricultural college in England and was established under the patronage of Prince Albert. The cost of construction was £3,674. A chapel was added in 1847–8. Its royal charter stated that the college was 'for teaching the science of agriculture, and the various sciences connected therewith, and practical application thereof to the cultivation of the soil, and in the rearing and management of stock'. Interestingly, the college also had a museum 'which contains many excellent anatomical, botanical and geological specimens and is also replete with the results of chemical analysis and articles of interest in each department taught'. Its contents have long since been dispersed. *(postmarked 1904: H.W.Taunt)*

Cirencester Cottage Hospital in Sheep Street. (*W. Dennis Moss*)

In 1895 the town's Friendly Societies inaugurated a hospital demonstration and raised modest sums ranging from £7 to £19 a year. In 1900 the Friendly Societies' Hospital Carnival was started, and the carnival became an annual fundraising event. Here is one such parade passing through the Market Place.

Cirencester Cottage Hospital in Sheep Street, built by Allen Bathurst, was opened in March 1875 in memory of his first wife, the Hon. Meriel Leicester Warren, daughter of George, second Baron de Tabley. She died in 1872, six years before Allen Bathurst succeeded his uncle William Lennox as sixth Earl Bathurst in 1878. There had been some opposition to the scheme, but a committee formed to administer and raise funds emphasised it was 'designed for the benefit and accommodation of the poor when suffering from disease or accident which cannot be treated adequately in their own homes'. *(W. Dennis Moss)*

Seven beds were available and nursing staff dealt with an average of 138 patients per year, and about 200 outpatients. The chief sources of income were the annual subscriptions and the church and chapel collections on Hospital Sunday. The Cirencester Amateur Dramatic Club productions contributed other funds, and public subscription and personal donations, often listed in the newspaper, ranged from gifts of eggs, milk and turkeys to books and religious tracts.

Structural alterations and improvements provided an increased number of beds and a private room for the matron (1895); the garden was enlarged by the demolition of the old British School (1897); a nurse's bedroom was provided on the top floor (1899); a new operating theatre was equipped in 1901; and a new ward in 1904 expanded the number of beds to eleven. A new mortuary was built, and in 1911 a new veranda was added for the use of convalescents, paid for with funds raised by the Friendly Societies' Hospital Demonstration.

In 1911 admissions numbered 150, and, following the building additions funded by Bingham in 1913, the number of beds was increased to seventeen. Extensive work provided for improved wards and nursing facilities with new staff bedrooms, kitchens and bathrooms. Decorative refurbishment throughout was to a very high standard and electric light was installed by Messrs Edwards and Armstrong of the Cirencester Electric Lighting Company. The architect for the work in 1913 was V.A. Lawson, at a cost of £2,500, whereby the new hospital was doubled in size and praised for its light, airy and well-ventilated accommodation.

The *Wilts & Gloucestershire Standard* for 17 April 1913 reported, 'The Cirencester Hospital – the Institution has now grown to such dimensions that the adjective "Cottage" must be dropped from its title – was re-opened on Thursday last, after the enlargement by the munificence of the late Mr D.G. Bingham, the last generous gift of that large-hearted philanthropist to his native town.'

The Independent or Congregational Chapel in Wharf Road (renamed Sheep Street) was built in 1839. The congregation moved to a new chapel in Dyer Street, which opened in 1888, and the old chapel was renamed Apsley Hall and used for meetings and entertainments. Note a collection of road mender's handtools in the foreground, with a number of potholes still to be filled in.

Sheep Street, Memorial Hospital, *c.* 1925. Apsley Hall was converted in 1919 to house the X-ray equipment that had been installed in the Red Cross Hospital in the Bingham Hall in the First World War. The alterations overseen by V.A. Lawson included the commemorative plaques to the war dead, and the building was renamed the Memorial Hospital. (*W. Dennis Moss*)

*Walking south from the Market Place down
Cricklade Street to Ashcroft,
with a view from The Querns.*

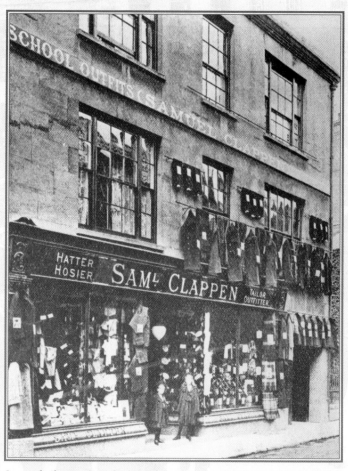

Samuel Clappen's tailor's and outfitter's shop in Cricklade Street,
now Ottakar's bookshop.

Above: Bishop's Corner, at the top of Cricklade Street, 1915. Troops stand outside the Bell Inn. Bishop's has closed pending demolition, and already its main advertising board has been removed. (*W. Dennis Moss*)

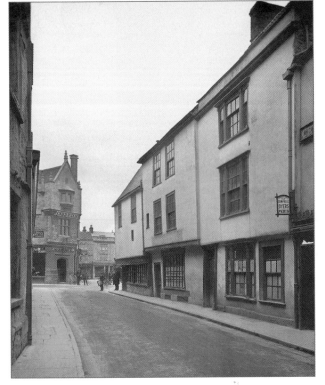

The same group of buildings seen from a little way into Cricklade Street. The sign for the Crystal sweet shop can just be made out on the right. Jettied and overhanging buildings such as these have largely disappeared from the Cirencester street scene, but many survived until the extensive rebuilding programme in the town in the later Victorian and Edwardian period, as so clearly seen elsewhere in this volume. (*W. Dennis Moss*)

Cricklade Street, looking up towards the Market Place. On the left is the Three Horseshoes Inn, with its distinctive lamp, and, beyond, the hanging sign for Thomas Mann furniture dealer. A young boy stands at the entrance into Cirencester Brewery. John Smith's seedsmen and corn dealer's small shop is on the right; this firm later expanded on this site, on the corner by the entrance into the King's Head Tap and hotel yard. Further up, Hiltons shoe shop boasts one of the town's largest hanging shop signs.

The top of the street on the left is dominated by the bulk of the old Bell Inn on the corner. It was in the yard behind that the Cripps family of Cirencester had their brewery. They are recorded as brewers in a 1820 directory and from 1847 the energies of Frederick Cripps were responsible for considerable development, with later expansion at the end of the century including buildings to the street frontage as shown here, where the boy is standing at the brewery entrance. The brewhouse and chimneys were features of the town skyline, although now long gone; in addition a large maltings, which does partially survive in converted form, was built further down Cricklade Street. By 1920, with ninety licensed houses, Cirencester Brewery Company was the largest of the brewers in the town and area. The business was sold in 1937 and the buildings above the Cricklade Street entrance were rebuilt into the present row of shops just before the outbreak of the Second World War. *(postmarked 1907: Cherry of Cirencester)*

Another long-established Cirencester pub in Cricklade Street was the Bishop Blaize, seen here before 1892 when the road was widened and the buildings set back and rebuilt. William Dean was proprietor at this time. The pub was probably named after Saint Blaize, the patron saint of woolcombers, a craft associated with Cirencester. It closed as a pub in the early 1960s. Note the hatchet sign hanging from the nearby property of John Henry Jackson, ironmonger and edge-tool maker.

Cirencester was certainly well served by public houses, inns and taverns, as befits a market town. Using trade directories in particular, it is possible to trace something of the history of each one and chart their rise and fall. Pigot's Directory, for example, lists thirty-three inns and taverns in 1830 (the year Bingham was born) and in one form or another several remain as pubs today (marked in italics):

Castle Street: *Three Compasses*, *Black Horse*, Three Cocks, King's Arms
Cecily Hill: Pack Horse, Dolphin
Cricklade Street: *Wheatsheaf*, Bishop Blaize, Three Horse Shoes, Bell
Gosditch/Dollar Street: Swan, *Crown*, Red Lion, Ram
Dyer Street (includes Market Place): Ship, Sun, *Fleece*, *King's Head*, White Hart, Nag's Head, *Waggon & Horses*, Bull, *Bear*, Booth Hall
Gloucester Street: Volunteer, Anchor, *Royal Oak*, *White Lion*, Duke of York
Park Lane: Barley Mow
Park Street: Phoenix
Thomas Street: Horse & Groom
Watermoor: Three Bottles

Kelly's Directory of 1906 lists a grand total of thirty-four inns, including those in Watermoor, plus a number of beer retailers, including two in Cricklade Street.

In one of his paintings, the artist John Beecham depicted the story of Bishop Hooper halting in front of the Bishop Blaize Inn (depicted in its medieval form) on his way to be burnt at the stake in Gloucester in 1555. John Hooper, a zealous Protestant reformer, was appointed bishop of the newly created Diocese of Gloucester in 1550. With the accession of the Catholic Mary Tudor in 1553, the situation was reversed and Bishop Hooper was burned as a heretic two years later. Foxe's *Book of Martyrs* records that Hooper passed through Cirencester on his way to the city. Under armed escort, the party stopped for refreshment, and the hostess of a certain inn, who had spoken against Hooper but who was now overcome at the thought of how he was about to suffer and of her past unkindness, pleaded for his forgiveness. This painting hangs on show in the Town Council Chamber in Dyer Street, the property of the Bingham Library Trust. (*W. Dennis Moss*)

The next group of buildings further down Cricklade Street, also recorded before the 1892 alterations. The dog-leg in the street is very apparent as is the 12ft width, which resulted in increasing traffic problems along this principal through-route in the town. Jackson's hatchet sign shows clearly. Perhaps the most interesting feature of this group is the obvious overhanging jetties of the buildings, unaltered for centuries. Across the street, much of this group of shops has since been rebuilt and set back. (*W. Dennis Moss*)

Much the same viewpoint after the rebuilding, in a Tudor style, with Jackson's shop the principal focus and a range of goods displayed outside his shop, *c.* 1903. Next door is Peckham's the butcher's (later Shilham's) and beyond is the small but decorative sign of the Bishop Blaize. This particular part of Cricklade Street has seen many changes: rebuilding once again of the same group in the late 1980s was followed by a disastrous fire on 10 January 2004, in which three shops were completely gutted.

Kelly's Directory of 1897 contains a reminder of just how busy this commercial heart of Cirencester was at that time. The group of shops on the right of this picture, for example, included at no. 159 Moulder & Arnold, grocers (whose gable end advertisement is more clearly visible on the earlier photograph opposite), at no. 157 William King, cook and confectioner, at no. 156 Edward Hapgood, baker, and at no. 150 Charles Stallard, Phoenix Fish and Game Supply Co. Ltd. Others were at no. 149 Henry Larner, rope and twine dealer and fishmonger, at nos 143–4 Cole & Tranter, butchers, and at no. 142 James Stevens, furniture dealer – small businesses all. *(probably H.W. Taunt)*

The bottom end of Cricklade Street just above the junction with Lewis Lane and Querns Lane. Railings protect the access into nos 74 and 76 on the left-hand side. Double gates protect the entrance into Cock & Bartholomew 'implement store' and the small sign above the doorway in the foreground advertises Frederick Pearce, chimney-sweep. Referring to making improvements to Cricklade Street, the *Wilts & Gloucestershire Standard* describes 'cottages in crowded courts off the narrow street which are happily disappearing'.

A rarely seen view of cottages in Lewis Lane at the bottom end of Cricklade Street before the whole area was rebuilt in 1889. Hayward's tiny shop is on the corner. This part of town had (and still has) a considerable number of almshouses, usually complete with commemorative and informative plaques. The terrace on the right of this photograph was re-endowed by William Lennox Bathurst in memory of his sister the Lady Georgiana Bathurst, who died on 27 March 1874. Close by, in Querns Lane, six almshouses were endowed by Thomas Brewin, a prominent Quaker, as a memorial to his wife Mary, who died in 1883.

Behind the photographer in the northern end of Watermoor Road are two groups of almshouses associated with the Bowly family. One group of eight was built by Christopher Bowly in 1826, and endowed in 1837. A strict teetotaller, Bowly Senior was also responsible for the construction of the Temperance Hall in Thomas Street in 1846. He died in 1851. In 1918 two semi-detached houses were added to the row, the gift of Sarah Bowly, the wife of Christopher Bowly of Siddington House (and the son of Bowly Senior).

Across Watermoor Road, a plaque records that 'These Almshouses were built in 1924 at the special desire of Mr Christopher Bowly born 1837 died 1922.' This too is an attractive row of six almshouses designed by Norman Jewson and built by Messrs Berkeley of Cirencester. Christopher Bowly had many skills: he was curator of Earl Bathurst's Museum, a member of the Board of Health, a town guardian, and chairman of the Highways Board and of the Old Age Pension Committee. He represented Siddington on the Cirencester Rural District Council when it was established in 1894; he was a Justice of the Peace, and became chairman of the Cirencester Bench. (*W. Dennis Moss*)

Opposite, bottom: Few photographs survive, but this view looking straight up Cricklade Street in February 1914 records Ashcroft House, on the corner of Cricklade Street and Querns Lane.

This was the home of the Cripps family, surrounded by 7 acres of orchards, pasture and pleasure gardens, extending westward to Sheep Street. It was sold to Earl Bathurst in 1847, and occupied by a succession of tenants until 1890, when William Cripps re-purchased it. Six acres were sold at the end of the nineteenth century which opened up the area for development as Ashcroft Road and St Peter's Road. Ashcroft House itself was demolished in the 1960s.

The railings on the extreme left are at the side of Chesterton Manor and opposite is the corner office of Henry Cole & Co., corn millers. On the opposite corner with Lewis Lane stands another rebuilt group of houses, this time in 1889 by their owner Earl Bathurst. (*J.H. Thomas*)

A fine view by J.H. Thomas seeking to capture the whole of the town, as seen from the fields to the west, just below the amphitheatre. Using the church tower as a fixed point, in the foreground are the railway pens of the cattle market; beyond, the yards and sidings of the Great Western Railway branch line run across the picture from right to left with the station to the left. The Ashcroft development is in the right background.

Transport is an appropriate theme for this photograph. Daniel Bingham was born at the beginning of the railway era; he made it his career, and from it he derived his fortune. In his early childhood in town Bingham would have watched the surveying of the line and the laying out of the yards of what became the Great Western Railway station at the foot of Tetbury Road. The line opened in 1841 and a few years later Bingham went to work there in his first job. However, road transport continued to be a principal form of movement for goods and people. In 1827 a completely new road to Cheltenham was opened along the Churn Valley, forming a newly engineered turnpike from the top of Gloucester Street. It remains a very familiar route today.

Carriers were of prime importance for goods transport, and over time Cirencester had a fair number, based at various points in the town. In 1822, for example, two firms competed for trade, William Budd and Tanner and Baylis, with waggons and vans, offering daily trips to London, Bath, Bristol and intermediate places. At other times, Martin Taylor in Gloucester Street despatched waggons to Bath every Tuesday morning at six, and to Gloucester every Saturday morning at four; while William Turner in Dyer Street sent waggons to Bath, Bristol and South Wales. Jos. Page's waggons left the Bear in Dyer Street for Ledbury, Hereford and all parts of the North of Wales.

Just off this picture to the right is the wharf and depot of the Thames & Severn Canal, which was opened to Cirencester by 1787 and survived in use until the 1920s. Virtually all its business was in goods, principally coal. Competition was such that the canal was bought out by its great rival the Great Western Railway in 1882. *(J.H. Thomas)*

The Ashcroft development, seen here looking east along Ashcroft Road towards Cricklade Street. In the distance is the chimney for the steam engine in Newcombe builders' yard. *(Cherry of Cirencester)*

One of the principal buildings in the St Peter's Road development was St Peter's Roman Catholic Church, seen here with the Presbytery alongside. Built in 1895–6 by A.J.C. Scoles, it replaced the earlier and smaller Catholic church in London Road. *(W. Stackemann & Co, Teddington, London)*

Cirencester wharf and the warehouse of the Thames & Severn Canal, seen here in two early twentieth-century views, by which time the heyday of canal transport was over and the wharf used for local traffic only. Frank Gegg & Co. was a coal and coke merchant based on the wharf. A delivery of some 37 tons of Staffordshire coal to the company on the narrowboat *Staunch* caused a flurry of activity, as well as a major write-up in the local paper, and is recorded here on 19 March 1904, the first

delivery of coal by canal through the Sapperton tunnel for some years. Gegg had three of his coal carts ready for the unloading, and a local farm waggon has also been brought into use. The warehouse stands behind, one of three built on this canal to an identical design. In the later picture, Gegg stands with his horse Joey and delivery cart No 5 on the canal weighbridge. He closed his business in 1921, which virtually brought the canal wharf to an end, and for the next few years he is listed as the agent of another Cirencester coal merchant based across the road at the railway coal wharf.

The western end of Querns Lane, close to the junction with Sheep Street and looking back towards Lewis Lane, *c*. 1900. Another rarely photographed view and one that looks very different today. The cottages on the right continue to provide a fixed point of reference. Beyond are the trees in the grounds of Querns Lane House, the home of the Brewin family. The wharf of the Thames & Severn Canal is close at hand, around the corner in Workhouse Lane, now Querns Road.

The Querns on the western side of town was essentially a small suburban estate when it was laid out in 1825–6 for Charles Lawrence, a local solicitor, and his wife Lydia, who was one of the Bowly family. The land was leased from the third Earl Bathurst. In design it was a large ornamental villa, with park-like gardens, lodges, stables, an avenue and a walled kitchen garden. It stands close to the Roman amphitheatre and is now part of Cirencester Hospital. This line drawing of about 1840 was printed and sold by Henry Smith, a printer in the town between 1839 and 1892, with premises in the Market Place and later in Lewis Lane.

5
WATERMOOR

Until the early nineteenth century Watermoor consisted of an area of low-lying, and sometimes watery, common land and waste ground to the south of the town. The moor is first recorded in the twelfth century and refers to a small sub-manor, the property of Walter de la More in the fourteenth century. In 1825 the income derived from the sale of 'certain waste lands' in Watermoor by the Town Commissioners helped to finance the clearance of the Market Place and the improvement schemes in the town centre.

At the beginning of the nineteenth century the two principal land-owning families in the town were the Bathursts and Masters, the Bathurst estates lying principally to the west and south, while the Master land lay to the east of the town. In successive generations the Bathurst family gave substantial acreages for public utilities and institutions, including the canal basin for the Thames & Severn Canal, the termini and track for both the Great Western Railway and the Midland & South Western Junction Railway; land for the Cottage Hospital (1875) in Sheep Street; and in Watermoor land for the gas works (1833) and Watermoor Church and School (1851 and 1854). To the west, land was provided for the cattle market (1867) and for Chesterton Cemetery (1871), while a complete farm was leased in 1847 as the site of the Royal Agricultural College, the first such college in England. Within the town, extensive rebuilding and renovation of old properties was a continuing Bathurst concern, making notable contributions to the townscape in all the main streets of the old town.

The Master family acquired the site of the Augustinian abbey, to the north of the parish church, in 1539, soon after the Dissolution, and their house and private grounds provided a parallel buffer to the east of the town. They owned comparatively little property in the core of the old town, their principal land-holding comprising large nursery grounds to the south of Querns Lane and Lewis Lane, colloquially known as the Leauses, and extending south into Watermoor.

Smaller suburban estates were established at the beginning of the nineteenth century for successful upper middle class professionals. Watermoor House, built for Joseph R. Mullings in 1824, and The Querns, built for Charles Lawrence in 1825, provided rural quiet in close proximity to the town. Ashcroft House and Chesterton Manor were anomalies to a certain extent, in that their extensive grounds were cheek-by-jowl with crowded alleys behind Castle Street and Cricklade Street.

With an expanding population in the 1850s the demand for additional housing could only be met satisfactorily by developing the former nursery grounds to the south of the town. The old town offered little scope, and the desire to reduce the overcrowding in courtyards and alleys and consequently to improve the living standards of the town's population led to the expansion of working-class housing, and the development of Watermoor.

In the 1850s the land between Lewis Lane and Cricklade Road was laid out for building and small plots of land were offered for sale to encourage the construction of substantial villas, large semi-detached houses and short terraces to attract home owners of the lower middle class, professional and commercial classes. New roads were surveyed and plots laid out in Tower Street (1853), Corin Street and New Road (renamed The Avenue and Victoria Road respectively, in 1859), Chester Street and Church Street (1861). At the southern end of this new development, land was made available for small working-class dwellings, providing homes for the substantial workforce employed by the Midland & South Western Junction Railway carriage works and industrial foundries which relocated to the south of the town.

In the 1870s land to the east of New Road was offered for sale, and one of the first arrivals was the new Upper School opened in 1881. The Cirencester Improved Dwellings Company was responsible for the development of terraced housing in Queen Street, Prospect Place and School Lane, and to satisfy the needs of an expanding suburb, a new church, school, shops and public houses were built within the growing community.

The *Wilts & Gloucestershire Standard* reported on 16 July 1881:

Improved Cottages. Cirencester Improved Dwellings Company have now nearly completed a first block of eighteen cottages in School Lane, which are built on an excellent principle, and are pleasantly and healthily situate, and the rent has been fixed at 3 shillings per week, including rates. The contractors for their erection are Messrs. L. Saunders & Sons.

As is often the way, the old town attracted the attention of the early photographers, eager to produce souvenir postcards for the growing number of tourists and visitors, to the detriment of the new suburb for which the photographic record is much less intensive.

Watermoor, including Watermoor Road, Lewis Lane & Victoria Road.

Bowly's Almshouses in Watermoor Road.

The church of Holy Trinity in Watermoor Road, a new church for a growing part of the town, and built in the characteristic Early English or Gothic Revival style. The population of Cirencester in 1841 was around 6,000, with the parish church capable of seating 1,518 in a jumbled mass of enclosed pews, galleries and open benches. The Revd William Powell, succeeding the Revd Mr Pye as incumbent in 1839, appreciated the need to build a new church or chapel-of-ease, to support the growing population of Watermoor, and, as the name suggests, to provide 'ease and comfort' for those living at some distance from the parish church.

Building work began in 1847, and the church was consecrated on 6 November 1851. Sir George Gilbert Scott, as architect, designed a model church according to the standards laid down by the ecclesiological movement: a steep roof, with tower set to one side, and a dark interior and decorated chancel. The church was built on land donated by Henry George, fourth Earl Bathurst, with costs covered by subscription from local families, including Master and Croome. The spire was added in 1852, paid for solely by the Hon. William Lennox Bathurst. One unusual feature is the orientation, which is south-north rather than east-west. As a chapel-of-ease, burials were not permitted, so that interment continued in the parish churchyard before the town cemetery was laid out at Chesterton in 1871.

The Cirencester Union Workhouse opened in 1837 to cover thirty-nine local parishes under the Poor Law Act of 1834. Each group of inmates was to be segregated and outdoor relief for the 'undeserving poor' was reduced in an attempt to discourage idleness. The standard workhouse plan shows an allocation of space into dormitories for children, able-bodied males, able-bodied females, the sick, aged and other impotent poor. Workhouses such as this were usually constructed in two-storey blocks, built around courtyards. The regime was remembered with little more than fear and trepidation.

A view across to Watermoor railway station from the gardens of the Infectious Diseases Hospital, which was established in 1878 by the Local Government Board (newly formed in 1876 to replace the Town Commissioners) in a pair of houses standing well to the south of the town, and close to the gas works of 1833.

The town was unaffected by the cholera epidemics of the 1840s and 1850s, but there was an outbreak of scarlet fever in 1870, which resulted in the deaths of fifty-five people. Defective housing, poor sanitation and a contaminated water supply were cited as the possible causes, and the Local Board initiated a wholesale review of public health reforms to improve the town's supply of clean drinking water and sewage disposal. The 1880s witnessed a flurry of pipe laying through the town, for water, sewage and gas.

The development of a school is another key indicator of community expansion. Watermoor National School, Church of England, was founded in 1853 for girls, and boys up to the age of seven. A letter to the local paper dated 1 November 1854 has the story:

> It is proposed to build additional School Rooms for infants and elder girls, to be supported by weekly payments of the children, and by annual subscriptions, in connection with the Church of the Holy Trinity, at Watermoor. For this purpose, Earl Bathurst has kindly given a sufficient quantity of land, in an eligible situation close to the church, and sums have been promised. A school has, for many months, been opened in a small cottage, which numbers sixty children on its books, but it is impossible to admit other applicants without enlarged school rooms and a professed Mistress. To extend the means of Education in the Religion of the Church of England, and in industrial and other secular training, as above related, to the class of children whose parents can afford to pay, beyond that provided in the existing school where no charge is made.

By 1906 the average attendance was 133 girls and 96 infants. The school continues to thrive today.

Opposite, top: Lewis Lane, 1909. This shows the Cirencester Board School for Boys, Girls and Mixed Infants, opened in 1879, a year before education was made compulsory. It was built at a cost of £8,000 and enlarged in 1895 at a cost of £1,600. Designed to take 700 children, in 1906 the average attendance was 296 boys, 156 girls and 100 infants. Local School Boards were empowered to levy a rate to provide free elementary education, regardless of denomination. *(postmarked 1904: Cherry of Cirencester)*

Opposite, bottom: Looking eastwards in Lewis Lane, this delightful view of street activity involves groups of children who might well have just left the school further along the street. The Twelve Bells Inn is on the right, the turn into Tower Street visible beyond and two groups of almshouses stand on the left. A tradesman pushes a handcart along the street.

The Grammar School in Victoria Road, *c.* 1904. The original school building was in Park Lane, and was founded by John Chedworth, Bishop of Lincoln, in 1460, though further endowed by Thomas Ruthall, Bishop of Durham, a native of Cirencester, in 1508. The school moved to these newly built premises in Victoria Road in 1881. A report in the *Wilts & Gloucestershire Standard* in July that year reported,

Boys' Upper School, Cirencester. The spacious and handsome new school, authorised by the new scheme under which Powell's charity is now governed, and which has for sometime past been in course of erection in the New Road, is now rapidly approaching completion, and does credit alike to Messrs Waller & Son, of Gloucester, the architects, and Mr William Hinton, of Cirencester, the contractor. The school which will accommodate 110 pupils, will be opened at Michaelmas next, the fees being £6 per annum. The governors have unanimously appointed the Revd G.R. Faulkener as their first head master under the scheme.

With later additions in 1899 (the 'boys' end to the south) and 1904 (the 'girls' end to the north) the school expanded to provide room for 200 pupils. In 1904 the Cirencester High School for Girls was incorporated into the Grammar School and moved from The Avenue to Victoria Road. *(W. Dennis Moss)*

The southern end of Victoria Road at the junction with Queen Street, *c.* 1910. Built as New Road and laid out in 1859 as a significant development on this side of town, it was later renamed in 1887 to mark the Golden Jubilee of Queen Victoria. The coal cart is delivering bushel baskets of coal to Andrews Bakery on the corner of Queen Street. The wooden picket fence is at the corner of the post office.

Above: Cirencester had two stations once the Midland & South Western Junction Railway (MSWJR) had opened its station at Watermoor in 1883. This cross-country route linking the south coast ports of Southampton and Portsmouth to the industrial north via Cheltenham competed with the GWR for much of its life. A substantial railway depot was established in Watermoor in 1895, with extensive yards and workshops for locomotives and carriage building. The company provided considerable local employment until closure of the works in 1925. The station closed in 1961.

Among the social activities of the MSWJR works was a brass and reed band of some thirty members, formed in 1903 under bandmaster James Tyrrell. It was much in demand, entertaining at the invitation of Rajah Charles Brooke in the grounds of Chesterton House, for example, and on summer Saturday evenings it also performed in the Market Place. The band played on more formal occasions such as the coronation celebrations of King George V on 22 June 1911, when it gave a full programme throughout the day. In this view of Railway Sunday in 1908 the band leads the parade along Watermoor Road, with the railway bridge in the background.

Interior view of Jukes Foundry in Watermoor, 1912. John Delve came from Devon to manage Alexander's foundry in Cricklade Street, which had been established by Henry Alexander in 1849. Delve acquired the business in 1883 and moved it here to Watermoor. The foundry was later purchased by Samuel Jukes in the early 1900s, and he in turn sold it in the 1930s to Fred Hope, who is remembered as its last owner.

Cirencester was long renowned for the manufacture of edge-tools, agricultural implements and machinery. There were foundries in Cricklade Street, Dyer Street and the Suffolk Ironworks in Lewis Lane. Webbs in Gloucester Street also made agricultural implements. Wholesale ironmongers included Alexander & Thompson (where Woolworths is now) and Gillman's in Black Jack Street, which only recently closed down.

A trade postcard, postmarked 1909, on behalf of F.W. Andrews & Co, General Supply Stores of 13 Watermoor Road, festooned with enamel advertising signs.

6

THE BINGHAM HALL
& RIFLE RANGE

Bingham's second major gift to the town was the Bingham Public Hall and Rifle Range, constructed in King Street in 1908. V.A. Lawson was the architect for this project, and the builders, Messrs Orchard and Peer of Brimscombe, completed the work in less than a year.

Bingham purchased the large plot of ground at Watermoor which originally formed part of the Watermoor House estate, and which, possessing an area of nearly 5,500 square yards, and frontage to both Watermoor Road and the newly constructed thoroughfare called King Street, afforded an admirable site for the purpose, being in the middle of the large and growing population in the Watermoor district which is practically the only direction in which the town is likely or able to extend its borders.

In digging the hall foundations the remains of a Roman building, most probably a winged-corridor house, were exposed lying to the east of the line of Ermin Street, the principal north-south Roman road through the town.

A piece of Roman pavement was discovered on the site of the building, and Mr Lawson had this carefully removed and prepared by Messrs. Turpin and Co., the experts in Mosaic work, for insertion in the Terrazzo floor of the office and cloak room at the principal entrance, affording both an interesting souvenir of old Corinium, and a curious instance of the combination of the ancient and modern in industrial art.

The foundation stone was officially laid by Countess Bathurst on 7 March 1908. A large crowd assembled while the Midland & South Western Junction Railway Works Band, under bandmaster R.H. Lewis, played a selection of tunes. Daniel Bingham was represented by his nephew, Frederick.

Bingham was motivated in part by the 'importance of doing something for the boys of the town in whose hands the future so largely lies'. The Bingham Library provided instruction and educational facilities for adults and special arrangements for girls.

Bingham was impressed with the vital importance of providing the boys of Cirencester with the means and inducement for spending their evenings in healthful and wholesome pursuits and recreation, instead of wasting their time in street loitering, which often degenerates into even more distinctly injurious habits.

The foundation of the two Lads' brigades in the town, the First Cirencester Company of the Boys' Brigade and the Cirencester Company of the Church Lads' Brigade (with its subsequently added Cadet Corps) was viewed by Mr Bingham with supreme satisfaction and each organisation received his substantial support. In the Hall now being built his design is to provide headquarters for these bodies, as well as facilities for promoting the healthy development and exercise of the youthful male population of the town.

With the threat of war not far away on the horizon,

Mr Bingham heartily shares the zeal and enthusiasm with which Field Marshal Lord Roberts is seeking to encourage the young men of England to qualify themselves for taking a hand, should need arise, in the defence of their hearths and homes, and he therefore conceived the idea of establishing the Cotswold Rifle Club for the promotion of the practice of the art of rifle shooting.

The hall is larger than the Corn Hall, capable of seating 800 to 1,000, with a large stage and proscenium and adjoining ante-rooms and dressing rooms. The Rifle Range ran the whole 100ft length of the hall and was equipped with all the latest equipment, including a Solano target.

The Hall was to be used for Drilling, Rifle Practice, Gymnastics, Games, Lectures, Readings, Concerts, Dances, Dramatic and other Entertainments, Flower, Poultry and other Shows as the Trustees and Board of Governors may from time to time think fit.

The building was formally opened by Mrs Bingham on 14 October 1908, followed by a two-day fancy fair held in the hall in aid of funds for the restoration of the Town Hall, and for purchasing and pulling down shops in West Market Place in order to open up the west end of the church. Mrs Bingham presided over a stall of Dutch items, which attracted considerable interest.

On display during the Fancy Fair, paintings on framed Dutch tiles, including two peculiarly handsome ones on richly carved easels. One of these, and several of the smaller ones, were paintings showing a portion of the ornamental water at Mr Bingham's Dutch shooting box, Schoonauwen, with a glimpse of the residence, while in a boat were seated Mr & Mrs Bingham and their niece.

Schoonauwen was a shooting box, 8 miles from Utrecht, where Bingham enjoyed the leisurely pastimes of shooting and fishing. The building, on a small island surrounded by a lake, was the ruined tower of an old feudal castle. The tile painting hangs now in the foyer entrance to the Bingham Hall.

Major Chester-Master was accorded the privilege of firing the first shot in the rifle range, and within the first weeks of opening a performance of *A Runaway Girl* was staged to test the acoustics, 'should there be a need to amend the ceiling'. The necessary amendments were made and the hall has been host to a multitude of plays, concerts, and entertainments ever since.

As with the library, Bingham erected, equipped and endowed the hall and appointed Trustees to oversee its future management. Earl Bathurst was president with the Hon A.B. Bathurst as vice-president; F.W. Woods acted as secretary and treasurer to fellow Trustees Archdeacon Sinclair, Edward Blundell, William Cole and Robert Ellett. As architect, Lawson

designed not only the Hall and Rifle Range, but also a caretaker's dwelling, together with twelve cottages fronting King Street and six villas fronting Watermoor Road, the rental derived from these houses being intended by Mr Bingham to form a revenue for the upkeep of the Institution.

The whole forms a distinctive group, giving King Street a special character.

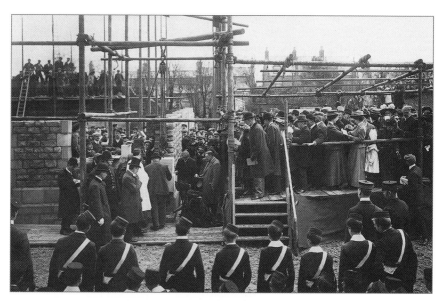

Countess Bathurst laying the foundation stone of the Bingham Hall in King Street on 7 March 1908. A Moss postcard of the scene was quickly available; one was sent on 13 May to a local girl away in service with the message 'What do you think of this?' (*W. Dennis Moss*)

The opening ceremony of the Bingham Hall performed by Mrs D.G. Bingham on 14 October 1908. (*W. Dennis Moss*)

The Bingham Hall as completed in 1908, in the newly laid out King Street looking towards Victoria Road. *(W. Dennis Moss)*

An interior view of the new Bingham Hall in 1908, looking towards the stage. This view is valuable in that it shows the roof design before it was altered soon after opening in order to improve the acoustics. *(W. Dennis Moss)*

The Rifle Range and Armoury in 1908. The commemorative booklet reports that 'the range is 100ft in length though the targets and firing arrangements can be adjusted for the use of any visiting teams who may be accustomed to firing at shorter distances. In addition to the ordinary bulls-eye targets (eight in number) there is a Solano target with varied landscape and moving figures.' *(W. Dennis Moss)*

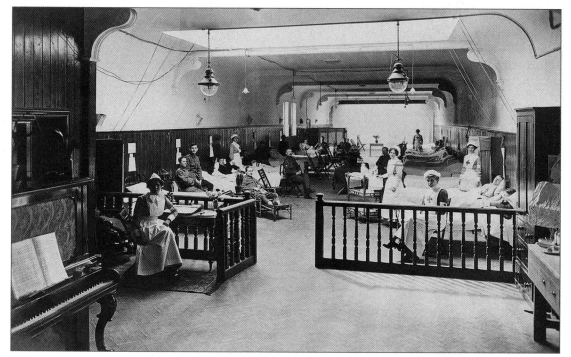

During the First World War, the hall was used as a Red Cross hospital. Patients were brought by train to the MSWJR station in Watermoor before being transferred to the hall. This view shows the rifle range. *(W. Dennis Moss)*

In this aerial view of the southern part of Cirencester and much of Watermoor in the 1950s there is much to pick out and examine. Holy Trinity Church in Watermoor Road can be seen, and so too the obvious change in direction as Watermoor Road leaves the town en route for Cricklade and Swindon. Obliquely at an angle, Victoria Road dominates the right of the picture, as it does the whole development of this area. The Bingham Hall stands out in King Street. Not least, the MSWJR tracks sweep across the picture and into Watermoor station (then still in use). The breaks in the terraces of houses clustered around it show how effectively the building of this line cut across the intended development plans. The gas works can also just be seen at bottom left. The former railway works stand pretty much abandoned; the present day town fire station and roundabout fill much of this space. Of the open spaces shown here, the best preserved remains the large rectangular area just north of King Street, now St Michael's Park.

In the period covered by this volume, and since, this whole area has undergone considerable change more than once. Bingham witnessed a great deal of change in the historic centre of Cirencester, and would have been aware of developments to the south and in Watermoor. Later, in the middle decades of the twentieth century, further substantial changes occurred. The Love Lane industrial estate was established, and has since become a central feature of the town's commercial life. The long-planned ring road and bypass route around the town dramatically altered the Watermoor landscape, one transport network (railway) giving way to another (road). Once again roads dominate our lives, as they did when Bingham was born in Cirencester in 1830.

ACKNOWLEDGEMENTS & FURTHER READING

The compilation of a volume such as this relies upon the goodwill of a great many people, and it is a delight for the compilers to acknowledge that the sharing spirit, which is such a hallmark of local history research, has been very evident in this project.

Conceived as part of the ongoing work of improving access to the Bingham Library Trust's cultural assets in all their variety, the volume is largely drawn from the photographic and picture collections of Trust material held in the Bingham Library. Unless otherwise stated, all material reproduced here comes from that source. Particular thanks are due to Gloucestershire County Council, the staff of the Bingham Library and the Gloucestershire Record Office. The work of individual photographers is acknowledged in the text where known, from which it will be seen how great is the significance of W. Dennis Moss's output of Cirencester and south Cotswold images over many years from his studios in Castle Street. No less important, but rather less well known, is the carefully documented archive of the J.H. Thomas collection, gifted to the Trustees in 1954. Verification of unacknowledged images to known photographers would be welcomed.

Many people have exercised their professional skills of caring for these collections, principally the generations of librarians of the Bingham Library. In so doing they have added their own additional information and strengthened the whole. Although it may be invidious to mention specific names, the late G.P. Jackson was librarian for some thirty-five years, 1935–70, and to him fell the challenges of care and continuity through and beyond the war years of 1939–45. On behalf of the Gloucestershire County Library, Alan Welsford maintained that fine tradition, and a number of members of staff developed particular research interests in the collections, especially Trevor Allen on J.H. Thomas and the late Jean Welsford, whose role as Local Historian in Residence was a most welcome, if tragically short-lived, development. Jean's *Cirencester in Old Photographs* album in 1987 drew upon the same collection as this present volume, and a number of the best from her selection are reproduced again here.

Present day library staff continue to offer skilled care and oversight, albeit within storage and access conditions that are becoming increasingly cramped. Throughout, and in one form or another over the past century since 1905, the Bingham Library Trust has retained ownership responsibility of its collections and has authorised a range of funding improvements over the years. Development plans show how this is intended to continue into the future. Trustees past and present as well as officers of the Trust are warmly thanked for their contributions to this process.

Today's local historians and collectors have added additional material to greatly enhance the flow of the volume in its tour of the town. June Stacey (pp. 19 and 138 upper), Peter Grace (pp. 50 and 140), Philip Griffiths (pp. 59 upper, 70, 77 lower, 101, 103 lower, 104 upper, 106 lower, 108 lower, 109, 110 lower, 113, 117, 122 upper and lower, 124 upper, 131 lower and 132 lower), Edwin Cuss (pp. 104 lower,

107, 133 lower and 137 upper), Bunie Loveridge (pp. 127, 129 upper and lower, 133 upper and 134 upper) are all especially thanked, in each case for their long-term support as well as specific interest via loans of selected items for inclusion in this volume. Cirencester Archaeological & Historical Society kindly made 59 lower, 74 upper and 123 lower available. To enhance the sequence other material has been drawn from the compilers' own collection (pp. 32 upper, 77 upper, 96, 97, 123 upper and 134 lower).

Permission to quote extensively from the pages of the *Wilts & Gloucestershire Standard* was kindly given by the editor, Peter Davison. The key issues are 23 January 1904 (laying of Bingham Library foundation stone), 23 September 1905 (opening ceremony), 8 March 1913 (Bingham's obituary) and 17 October 1908 (opening of Bingham Hall). Peter Grace (since the year 2000) and Gerry Stribbling (for ten years previously) have maintained a weekly 'Nostalgia' and 'The Way We Were' section in the pages of this newspaper, which has achieved the status of a substantial archive of town history and the recorded memories of its citizens. Long may it continue. As if in recognition of this being a continuous process, outside the window as this book was being assembled and written, demolition began on Cirencester's Regal Cinema, opened in 1937 and closed in November 2003 – but certain to be fondly remembered locally for many years to come.

All in all, as the bibliography suggests, Cirencester has been fortunate in its historians, although there remain some substantial gaps in the overall research output. It seems appropriate to conclude this particular album with an acknowledgement to some of the principal names over the past three centuries: Sir Robert Atkyns, Samuel Lysons, Samuel Rudder, the Revd E.A. Fuller, W.K. Beecham, K.J. Beecham, W.St.Clair Baddeley, W. Scotford Harmer, Bob Jennings and Jean Welsford. To those accessing the reference collections now and in the future these names will crop up time and again, which is as it should be.

The greatest source of contemporary town life is to be found in the pages of the *Wilts & Gloucestershire Standard*, founded in 1837 and still going strong. The local history columns 'Nostalgia' and more recently 'The Way We Were', which have run since 1990, provide an excellent assemblage of memorabilia, fact-finding and social record.

The format of this book as a walk around Cirencester mirrors that of the long-standing publication *Cirencester: a Town Walk*, published and promoted by Cirencester Civic Society (latest edition, 2003), and the two might usefully be followed in parallel. *The Cirencester Experience* by Miriam Harrison and Shirley Alexander (Reardon Publishing, 1998) offers another way of seeing the town on foot and with fresh eyes.

For more detailed background study, the following is a summary list of the most useful publications on the town's more recent history, excluding the detailed archaeological reports on Cirencester's Roman, Anglo-Saxon and medieval past. Copies are available for study on request at the Bingham Library.

The local history collections include photographs, original documents, copies of the census, parish records etc and are available for study on request in the Bingham Library.

Baddeley, W. St. Clair, *The History of Cirencester* (Cirencester, 1924)

Bartholomew, D., *Midland & South Western Junction Railway*, vol. I (Wild Swan Publications, 1982)

Beecham, K.J., *History of Cirencester and the Roman City of Corinium* (1st edn, 1887; facsimile reprint with introduction by David Verey, Alan Sutton, 1978)

Bray, N., *The Cirencester Branch* (Oakwood Press, 1998)

Cuss, E., *The History of Cirencester Grammar School by John Ireland* (n.d., but 1994), and *Looking Back at Cirencester Grammar School* (Cirencester, 1996)

Cuss, E. & Griffiths, P., *The Churn, Coln and Leach Valleys in Old Photographs* (Alan Sutton, 1990)

——, *Around Cirencester in Old Photographs* from the W. Dennis Moss Collection (Alan Sutton, 1991)

Darvill, T.C. & Gerrard, C., *Cirencester: Town and Landscape* (Cotswold Archaeological Trust Ltd, 1994)

Emson, S. & Bull, M. (eds), *Cirencester*, Ottakar's Local History (Tempus, 2002)

Harmer, W.S., *Cirencester Present and Past, Old Streets and Houses*, in Baddeley, 1924, 309–328.

Hawkins, B., *Taming the Phoenix: Cirencester & the Quakers 1642–1686* (Sessions of York, 1998)

Loveridge, G.G., *Watermoor Through the Ages: Reflections on a Cirencester Community over 150 Years* (Cirencester, 1977)

McWhirr, A.D. (ed.), *The Archaeology and History of Cirencester*, British Archaeological Abstracts 30 (Oxford, 1976)

Reece, R. & Catling, C., *Cirencester: the development and buildings of a Cotswold town*, British Archaeological Abstracts 12 (Oxford, 1975)

Rudder, S., *The History of the Antient Town of Cirencester*, 'printed and sold by S. Rudder, Dyer Street, Cirencester; sold also by T. Stevens, in the Market-place', 1800

Turner, K. & Berkeley, B., *A Narrow Cotswold Street: Coxwell Street, Cirencester*, Coxwell Street Residents Assn (Cirencester, 2000)

Verey, D. & Brooks, A., *Gloucestershire: The Cotswolds*, Buildings of England series (Penguin Books, 1999)

Viner, D. J., *Cirencester As It Was* (Hendon Publishing, 1976)

——, *The Thames & Severn Canal History & Guide* (Tempus, 2002)

Welsford, J., *Cirencester: a History and Guide* (Alan Sutton, 1987)

——, *Cirencester in Old Photographs* (Alan Sutton, 1987)

Apart from the material known to be in the copyright ownership of the Trust, every attempt has been made to seek out and acknowledge copyright holders of other images used here; any omissions are unintentional and the compilers, the Trustees and the publishers would be pleased to hear of any errors or omissions for correction in any future edition.

David & Linda Viner

The compilers of this album are both well-known town historians in Cirencester. David was Curator of the town's Corinium Museum for twenty-seven years and has written and compiled ten books and albums on local life, Cotswold social history and the Thames & Severn Canal. He is Chairman of Cirencester Archaeological & Historical Society. Linda is an historical researcher, with an especial interest in Cirencester over many years. Together they act as curatorial advisers to the Trust and have jointly researched and compiled this book for the Trustees.

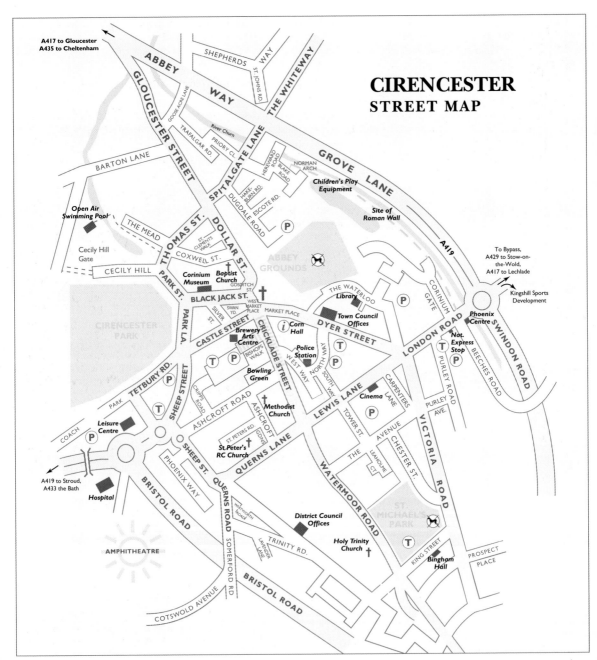

CIRENCESTER
STREET MAP

Based upon the Ordnance Survey mapping with the permission of the Controller of Her Majesty's Stationery Office. Crown copyright reserved. © Drawn by The British Publishing Company Limited, Gloucester 1994 © DMC Revised 2001.